MIGRATION

MIGRATION
From Massachusetts Bay
to the Old Northwest
1636 – 1836

RICHARD RAWSON

E.L.F. BOOK ENTERPRISES
ALEXANDRIA, VIRGINIA

This work is dedicated to the memory of Harold and Robert Rawson, brothers who shared a love of history and family, and who spent their retirement years collaborating in exploring their roots.

It is written for Emerson, Lincoln and Franklin Rawson, thirteenth generation descendants of Secretary Edward Rawson of the Massachusetts Bay Colony, to help them understand their heritage.

CONTENTS

INTRODUCTION

E very family in America is a migration story. Whether the tale begins in Massachusetts Bay in 1636, or on Ellis Island in 1896, or in El Paso in 2006, or on the Beringian land bridge from Asia sixteen thousand years ago, we are all sons and daughters of immigrants. And most of us live today far from where our ancestors first set foot on the North American continent. Early on, people moved to find fertile hunting and trapping grounds or to secure cheap land to farm or to engage in trade. Some were fleeing restrictive religious authorities or oppressive political regimes. Others yearned for riches in gold rushes or silver mines. Many sought a new place simply to have a better chance to put food on the table for their children. And there were always those who needed to escape the consequences of their own mistakes and find a fresh start.

How many ancestors, how many threads are there in the family story of any one of the 330+ million of us in the United States today? Take a young person born at the turn of the 21st century. At the time of the Civil War, she would have 64 direct ancestors. Turning the clock back to the American Revolution, more than 500 people would have contributed their DNA to her. And if she can trace her American ancestry back to the time of Jamestown and Plymouth, she would be the cloth of more than 10,000 interwoven strands. Each of these threads, her ancestors, had a story of his or her own, mostly unknowable to us today.

If we could somehow magically retrieve all of the information about the travels of individuals and their families from their progenitors' first places to the present, we could construct a beautiful and compelling picture, a meta-view, of the flow

of people from coastal settlements to interior farm communities, from tightly packed villages to open hills, across mountain
passes and over inland lakes and great plains to populate coastal
settlements once more. Some of the streams would stop and
start, twist and turn slowly through generations of individual
decisions. Others would lead more directly and inexorably west
as native peoples, earlier immigrants themselves, were pushed
aside or driven away or ruthlessly hunted down. Many of the
streams would loop around on themselves, bringing people
back to the east or even migrating back out of the United States
altogether.

　　We would see the first trickle of royalists, adventurers, inden-
tured servants and enslaved Africans into Virginia start to flow
toward the Alleghenies and the Appalachians, be held back for
a time by the French with their forts and their native allies, and
then break the dam and spill into what became Ohio, Kentucky
and Tennessee, increasing their numbers vastly as Scotch-Irish
poured into the colonies in the years just before the Revolution.
We would see Puritans and others spreading from Massachusetts
Bay and the Connecticut River valley down to Rhode Island and
Long Island, and up into Maine, New Hampshire and Vermont,
with their descendants traversing Lake Ontario and Lake Erie by
sail or steam to the Old Northwest Territory.

　　Dutch and Swedes and Germans as well as English would
travel up the Hudson and the Delaware and the Susquehanna
Rivers before turning west to New York's Genesee Valley and
other lands made accessible after wars and treaties and more wars.
French traders at first and displaced English Tories later would
populate the St. Lawrence River valley and the northern side
of the Great Lakes. Spanish, Mexican and mestizo immigrants
would settle habitable patches of the North American southwest
and the beginnings of California.

　　Technology would play a huge role in making these migrations possible. Covered wagons and canals, sailing ships and
steamboats, roads and rails and labor-saving farm equipment
from iron plows to threshing machines would all help to impel

people westward. So, too, would economic factors including land speculation, banking and capital aggregation in joint stock companies, the opening of new markets and new trade routes, and even the vicissitudes of fashion in Europe which affected the demand for North American fur.

No complete account can be given of all of the individual choices and family decisions to pick up and move, to join the flows of migration that have in turn created the complex, multi-layered history of our country. Biographers, to be sure, can sometimes provide a textured view of a person or even of a family in their particular historical context. Genealogists can reconstruct the linked chain of lives across decades or even centuries. And a number of prominent migration historians have done an extraordinary job of delving into records, documenting migration forces and trends, and creating analytical paradigms to explain the movement of peoples. But there appears to be a gap in explanations of how these migration forces and trends played out in the lives of particular families over a period of centuries.

Why did a specific person or family move from here to there at a given point in time? What drove them to take the risks? Why did their children and their children's children then stay there? And why of a sudden did a next generation choose to pick up and move when they did and where they did? And move again. And again. And why then did four or five or more generations of the same family stay rooted in the same place when neighbors as well as transient strangers created a powerful groundswell to move on to the next promised land?

A complete such tale is the stuff of novels or of scripture, for the historical record for almost any family is too fragmented, incomplete and ambiguous to yield all of the insights we would wish to have. Only a fortunate few have ancestral letters or memoirs or biographies to explain some part of their family's past. But piecing together even a partial view of a family's history in the framework of what was happening in its time—politically, economically, socially—is an exercise that can illuminate certain elements of at least one current, in one stream, of the broader flow of history. As James Baldwin wrote, "the past is all that can make the present coherent."[1]

This is an account of how the unfolding of English and American history affected ten generations of one branch of a particular American family, the Rawsons. Their story began with a voyage from the south of England across the broad Atlantic to the Massachusetts Bay Colony in the 1630s, expanded into the dangerous frontier in Mendon, Massachusetts fifty years later, ventured north to hilly lands made safe by the Revolutionary War in Pittsford, Vermont in 1800, and then leaped hundreds of miles in a single generation to the newly organized territories of the Old Northwest in Milan, Michigan in the 1830s. And then they stopped when so many others pressed on.

Why? What social, political or economic factors were at work to push or pull the Rawsons? By what means were they able to make their way into new lands? What, if anything, connected them to the particular new lands they chose? Why did they come and go and stay as they did?

This Rawson story contains no presidents or generals, no bishops or business barons, and only one figure whose life left a few significant historical footprints. These Rawsons were, for the most part, just the average farmers or carpenters, lawyers or accountants or engineers whose kind have made up so much of the middle class of generations of Americans. But, collectively, these Rawsons provide a vantage point from which large parts of the early history of America can be viewed, at least as they experienced it.

This is their migration story.

---

[1] Baldwin, *Collected Essays*, p. 7.

PROLOGUE

Edward Rawson

Edward Rawson, Secretary of the Great and General Court of the Massachusetts Bay Colony, tossed another log on the fire and returned to his writing desk. A pile of petitions, resolutions and orders from the just concluded Court session in 1667 sat on a corner of the desk, waiting for his signature and the Court's seal. He returned to the petition he had put aside to tend the fire and looked again at the land survey for which approval was sought, as well as the names of the petitioners: Cook, Thayer, Smith, Aldrich, White, Lovett and others. Secretary Rawson knew something of these men.

Many of them were from Weymouth, not far from Boston on the south side of the bay. These were West Country men whose families had come to New England from Dorsetshire, just as he had more than thirty years ago. They were solid, hardworking yeomen, as were the families from next door Braintree joining them in the petition. If anyone could make a success of a new settlement, he knew they could. Over the last eight years, they had successfully petitioned the Court for permission to seek out a place for a "new plantation," received approval for the site, obtained deeds from the Nipmuc natives of the area, drawn up rules for governance of the settlement and begun to move their families.

What drives this appetite for new lands, for new settlements farther and farther from Boston? the Secretary might have wondered to himself. *With the comforts of civilized society here in the Bay, and with the hardship of settling the tangled forests beyond, why would anyone cast their lot in the wilderness?*

And yet he knew that the migration beyond the coastal towns had started as soon as the Colony itself was founded. The masses of the Winthrop Fleet could not, would not all find their places in the towns springing up around the Charles and Mystic Rivers and up and down the Bay in the years following the first landings in 1630. Some made their way to the Connecticut coast. Others settled south on the shores of Narragansett Bay and Long Island, or north on the Maine coast. And the petitions to the Court for permission to stake out new lands started filtering in almost as soon as the Court itself was created, long before Rawson moved from his north coast home in Newbury to the capital of Boston town and became Secretary in 1650.

Now, in 1667, the frontier extended west to the Connecticut River valley towns of Hartford, Springfield and Deerfield, several days ride from Boston. Disputes with the natives continued to be a problem for the settlers in some areas, but the colonists always seemed to be able to find natives willing to take their trade goods and sign away the land. Their numbers devastated by European diseases as well as by conflicts with the newcomers like the destructive Pequot War in 1637, some natives continued to live in settlements near the new towns. Others were driven away or simply moved on when they could without running afoul of other tribes defending their own hunting and planting grounds.

What is it about this area they call Mendon that is so attractive to the Weymouth and Braintree men? Rawson might have pondered.

The Court had approved the survey in its session today, and the Secretary duly signed and sealed the document before laying it aside for publication to the petitioners. Thirty or so miles southwest of Boston, level with Plymouth and not far from the Rhode Island lands settled by that troublesome Roger Williams decades before, this new plantation would bear watching. The Secretary had already received grants of land from the General Court from time to time as a part of his compensation. Perhaps he would request a grant near the new Mendon plantation if things went well there. He wouldn't want to move away from his comfortable Boston life, of course, but there was value in land. And he had a large family to look after. Some of them might want to seek their fortunes on the edge of the wilderness.

This Mendon plantation would bear watching, indeed.

I.
OUT OF ENGLAND
TO MASSACHUSETTS BAY

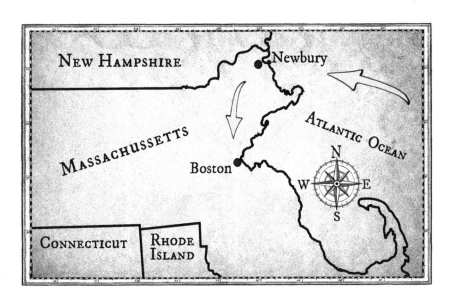

Kings once rode through the forest of Gillingham. The region had been conquered by the Roman Empire in the first century, later by Saxon tribes led by a chieftain named Ghylla (whose name endures), and then became part of the kingdom of Wessex as it fended off waves of Danish invaders. After the Norman conquest came the Angevin royal house of Henry II and Richard the Lionhearted. In the thirteenth century, Richard's brother and successor King John enjoyed the Gillingham forest so much that he had a royal hunting lodge built there, which was expanded by his son, Henry III. From the size and expanse of the long barrow-like mounds that are the only remains of this King's Court, historians conclude that a large stone and timbered lodge was set among outbuildings and stables for the royal retinues of dignitaries, soldiers and servants, all surrounded by a protective moat.

Over the centuries, the plentiful deer and stately oak trees of the Gillingham royal forest served a different purpose; though later kings and queens rarely visited the forest, they made gifts of its venison and timber for personal or political advantage. The forest also became a source of substantial revenue for the crown, as leaseholds were granted to tenants large and small, overseen by the king's appointed landlord or "Fee Forester." In the early seventeenth century, Charles I would ignite a firestorm of protests and violence by local farmers and herdsmen when he sent a royal commission to oversee the "disafforestation" of his Dorsetshire woodlands, raising fees and fencing off commonly used grazing meadows.[1]

Modern day Gillingham looks nothing like a royal hunting forest. A small town nestled along the River Stour in the north of Dorsetshire, a hundred miles southwest of London, Gillingham mixes Victorian era brick churches, shops and hotels with nondescript two- and three-story modern apartments, houses, commercial buildings and a train station. Sitting uneasily next to the large parking lot of a supermarket, two ancient thatched roof cottages are nearly hidden from view by hedges along a walking path to the town center. A small bridge across the several yard width of the Stour has replaced an ancient triple arched stone bridge so lovely that it drew the landscape painter John Constable to the area in the 1820s. The path leads into town past St. Mary's Parish Church, which has a history that runs back to Saxon days and still retains a chancel of medieval stonework.

Rawson Court stands just across a narrow street from the church yard, facing High Street, its entrance framed by eight foot high red brick pillars and black wrought iron fencing. The name, given both to an elder care facility housed in the stately Victorian manse that once served as St. Mary's vicarage as well as to the adjacent street and car park, pays homage to one of Gillingham's native sons, Edward Rawson. The young Rawson, born into a prosperous merchant tailor family well-connected to important Puritan clergy in England, left Gillingham around 1636 seeking opportunity just as thousands of others did by crossing the Atlantic to the far country of New England. He succeeded better than most, ascending to prominence as the Secretary of the Great and General Court of the Massachusetts Bay Colony and being reelected to that post each year from 1650 to 1686. By the time he died in 1693 in his comfortable home on Rawson's Lane near Boston Common, the Puritan immigrant Edward Rawson had given his family a new beginning.

* * * *

What does the fifteenth century "Most Serene Republic of Genoa" have to do with the Massachusetts Bay Colony and Edward Rawson? Genoa in 1450 may seem a strange place to begin to look for the roots of the migration of settlers in North America between 1636 and 1836. Perched on Italy's western coast at the top of the Ligurian Sea north of what is now called the Cinque Terre region, Genoa had declined from its status as a great power of the Mediterranean

in the thirteenth and fourteenth centuries to become a pawn
of France, Spain and Milan by the sixteenth. But Genoa's sea-
worthy ships and its skilled mariners played a prominent role
throughout those centuries, regardless of the ebb and flow of
alliances and wars it was forced to endure. Two of these mariners, Christopher Columbus and Giovanni Caboto (later called
John Cabot), both sea-faring sons of Genoa born just after 1450,
would play pivotal roles in what was to become a massive migration of humans two centuries later.

With the collapse of the Mongol Empire in the late 1300s,
the traditional land routes to the eastern sources of spice and
silk were closed to European traders. The search began for access
to the Indies by sea, led by the Portuguese Prince Henry the
Navigator in the fifteenth century. As his brave sailors worked
their way down the western coast of Africa looking for a route
to the eastern seas, others wanted to explore a direct route west
across the Atlantic to Cipangu and Cathay. Columbus, in particular, wandered the royal courts of Europe seeking a sponsor
for his "Enterprise of the Indies." He must have watched with
dismay as the successful eastward rounding of Africa's Cape of
Good Hope and return by Bartholomew Dias in 1487 ended any
chance of interesting the Portuguese.[2] But finding support, finally,
in Portugal's rivals Ferdinand and Isabella of Spain, the Genoan
Columbus opened the eyes of royal Europe to the opportunity
for riches by a western route. His four voyages between 1492 and
1504 planted the seeds of a Spanish empire in the New World,
even if Columbus himself never conceded that the lands he
explored were not the sought for Indies.[3]

The other Genoa-born mariner, Cabot, found his patron
in King Henry VII of England, who had turned Columbus
down but now grasped for a second chance at the western
opportunity. In 1497 Cabot made an extensive exploration of
Newfoundland far to the north of the lands "discovered" by
Columbus. Cabot brought home no gold or spices, but his
description of waters "brimming with cod in shoals so dense
they impeded the progress of his ship" led the fishermen of

England (as well as Portugal, Spain and France) to follow his path to the Grand Banks and other fertile fishing grounds of the western North Atlantic.[4]

Throughout the decades of the sixteenth century, other explorers crossed the Atlantic looking for riches or seeking the elusive sea route through the new lands and directly to the Indies. Giovanni Verrazano sailed for the French in 1524, investigating the North American coast from the outer banks of North Carolina, to the narrows of the great river later called the Hudson, to Maine and Newfoundland. Jacques Cartier (1534, 1535–36 and 1541–42) found and claimed for the French the lands north of Newfoundland up the St. Lawrence River as far as present day Montreal. For the English, Martin Frobisher (1576, 1577 and 1578), Sir Humphrey Gilbert (1579 and 1583) and John Davis (1585, 1586 and 1587) laid the basis for English claims to compete with the French in the far north of the New World, even as they failed to find the fabled Northwest Passage.[5] As the sixteenth century ended and the seventeenth began, Spain, England and France were joined by the Netherlands and Portugal in casting their mariners across the waters of the North and South Atlantic to search for gold and silver, fish and furs, and most of all—empire.

Voyages of discovery and exploration led to calls for colonization of the new lands claimed by England. Richard Hakluyt became a prominent voice for planting communities of Englishmen in the New World. His "A Discourse Concerning Westerne Planting," published in 1584, gave several reasons for England to look to the west, including the opportunities to extend the "Reformed Religion;" to avoid English dependence on other countries for trade; to employ the idle among a rapidly growing population; to counter Spanish expansion and power; and to discover the northwest passage to the Orient.[6]

Over the following decades, various versions of these arguments were used to convince the Crown to support establishing and expanding "plantations" in America. Native populations could be an ample source of new Christian converts, it was said, and their souls saved from the Spanish friars and French Jesuits preaching the unreformed Roman Catholic version of salvation. England was seen as too dependent on its trading partners, from the lumber and potash it needed from the Baltic countries, to the fish it bought from the Netherlands and Portugal, to the other foodstuffs it acquired from the European powers. The Spanish were an ever present threat, and English ports in America could be used to protect English ships and even to provide a springboard for taking away Spanish possessions in the West Indies. English power and prestige would be enhanced, the argument went, by increased lands, by growing its overseas population and by generating sources for trade with Englishman abroad. And the English held fast to the belief that gold and silver lodes must certainly exist in the northern reaches of the New World just as they did in the south, as well as to the inevitability that a Northwest Passage would be the English highway to the riches of the East.[7]

Royal patents were issued to would-be colonizers. A patent provided the legal basis for land ownership (and sale) as well as giving the holder exclusive rights to trade and to enjoy exemptions from customs duties for a period. Having a patent guaranteed none of these benefits, of course, and the flawed understanding of North American geography would combine with poorly drafted documents to create legal and physical disputes lasting decades, but the acquisition of a patent (or, later, a royal charter) was an essential beginning to any overseas enterprise.

Sir Humphrey Gilbert obtained a royal patent from Queen Elizabeth to found a colony in America in 1578, but failed to secure a foothold at Newfoundland. Sir Walter Raleigh championed early but also ultimately unsuccessful English efforts to plant colonies in North Carolina and Virginia in 1584 and 1585.[8] Martin Frobisher's contemporaneous efforts in Newfoundland suffered the same fate.

If English plans to colonize the New World were halting, the efforts to create a successful fishing enterprise were not. On a voyage to Newfoundland in 1583, Gilbert found dozens of fishing boats from several countries using the harbor at St. John.[9]

Historian Samuel Eliot Morison describes how the preferred English method of preparing the codfish catch ("dry" curing on land) required double crews, one to catch fish from small boats (or "shallops") and one to prepare and use the temporary wharves (called "stages") and drying platforms ("flakes") for curing the fish before shipment home.[10] This led to the creation of seasonal fishing camps, sometimes supplemented by attempts to grow crops for the fisherman and even to winter over on the rocky, unpromising coast. Key English port cities like Weymouth in Dorsetshire sent many of these fishing vessels to the cod banks each year as the sixteenth century turned into the seventeenth.

When Queen Elizabeth died without a royal heir in 1603, King James I (already King James VI of Scotland) ascended to the throne of England. Serious challenges, both domestic and foreign, confronted James. Many questioned his legitimacy, even to the point of plotting his removal or conspiring to blow him up in his Parliament building (the "Great Gunpowder Plot" of Guy Fawkes). Objections to his Scottish retinue and his Scottish religion left uncertainty and dissatisfaction among English nobility and clergy. His spendthrift and extravagant living caused further unease. James had little understanding of and even less use for a sharing of governmental power between Parliament and the Crown, thinking himself an absolute monarch like many others in Europe. His foreign policy, it soon became clear, would seek to balance relations with the Catholic kings in Spain and France even to the disadvantage of fellow Protestant rulers in other parts of Europe. This balancing act failed as England was dragged into the continental war (the "Thirty Years War") pitting Spain against France and the German principalities. Costly and poorly managed, the English military failures took a heavy toll on James and his subjects, as taxes were levied to pay the armies and to refill depleted royal coffers.

Charles I, who became king in 1625, reigned over even greater turmoil than had faced his father, ultimately resulting in civil war and the loss of his head. This deeply troubled environment of Old England—with crises of economics, religion, war and governance—set the stage for the colonization of New England.

The economy of England suffered greatly in the first decades of the seventeenth century. Poverty and inequality increased as the population rapidly expanded.[11] The international market for English cloth, an important industry and employer, collapsed in the 1620s, putting many people out of work across the country and creating a crisis of pauperism in the cities. The failure of harvests, especially in 1623 and 1630, led to hunger and widespread riots.[12] As summarized by the prominent migration historian Bernard Bailyn, it was a time of "plummeting wages, rising rents, widespread unemployment, increased vagrancy, and escalating food prices which led to near famine among the poor."[13]

Religious disputes under Charles further poisoned English politics and threatened the position, property and even the physical safety of the powerful. England's separation from the Vatican under Henry VIII and the battles between the temporarily ascendant Catholics of Queen Mary and the restored Protestants of her successor Queen Elizabeth had left the English ever fearful of popish resurgence, a fear inflamed by King Charles's marriage to the Catholic daughter of King Philip of Spain. Charles, always seeking order and obedience, created more problems for himself by trying to impose an English Book of Common Prayer on Scottish Presbyterians. But the punitive measures taken against the Puritans by Charles and his Archbishop of Canterbury, William Laud, did the most to sharpen the divisions in the Church and in the Parliament.

Puritans took John Calvin seriously when he wrote about shedding the material excesses of the Roman church and rejecting anything that interfered with the direct relationship between a man and his God. Stained glass, organ music, vestments, even the hierarchy of bishops, they felt, were unscriptural and unnecessary. The Bible was clear enough, especially as propounded by the lengthy sermons of university educated preachers. When the Church of England retained much of the ritual and regalia of the Roman Catholics, some Puritans chose to separate themselves from what they viewed as this ungodliness, and left England for Holland. But the vast majority stayed at home and sought to be left alone in their local congregations. In King Charles, however, they soon found that their insistence on purer religious ways was seen as disobedient, blasphemous and even treasonous. William Laud, first as the influential Bishop of London and later as the powerful Archbishop of Canterbury, led the King's efforts to purge the pulpits and the universities of Puritans, and required a return to vestments and approved liturgies. More Puritans began to contemplate migrating to a place where they could worship and live as they believed God required.

Amidst this economic and religious turbulence, the King's wars against Spain and France in 1626 and 1627 created the need for new taxes, which Parliament refused to approve. Like his father, Charles proceeded to raise money through many kinds of special levies without parliamentary approval (including such measures as the enclosure and leasing of royal forest lands in places like Gillingham, giving rise to spasms of violence by local farmers that would unsettle such areas for decades).[14]

Allegations of conspiracy and even treason led to crackdowns by the King's cronies in the Star Chamber and to the imprisonment of some parliamentary leaders. Finally, his frustration with Parliament's refusal to raise taxes and its continued insistence on its historic prerogatives led Charles to dissolve Parliament in 1629. It would remain dormant until briefly revived in 1640, when the King again needed help (and more tax revenues) to fight the growing rebellions in Scotland and Ireland.

This is the background against which the Great Puritan Migration of 1630–1640 and the beginnings of English colonialism in New England must be viewed, and provides part of the answer to the essential question, "Why did these people move?" In the parlance of migration historians, the waves of English resettlement to the west that would begin around 1620 combined all of the classic elements driving migration.[15] The *pull* of greater economic opportunity, of the potential for bettering their situation and of land ownership, drew many, especially from among the younger sons of large families. The *push* of religious and political conflict, and later of outright persecution, drove others to seek security and liberty out of the reach of repressive political and religious regimes.[16] And the *means* of relocating large numbers of people thousands of miles from home became available in the seventeenth century as seagoing ships provided fairly reliable if uncomfortable and occasionally still hazardous ocean passage,[17] and as capital accumulation through private investment in joint stock trading companies made such ambitious enterprises possible.[18]

Pull, push and means all came together at the same time in the early seventeenth century. And to that triad might be added another key factor: *connection*. People who emigrated often did so in the company of family or neighbors, or to follow relatives on the same path to the same destination.[19]

Most Americans today, even if they paid attention in school, probably have a simplistic, even cartoonish understanding of English colonization efforts: John Smith and Pocahontas in Jamestown after 1607; the Pilgrims and the first Thanksgiving at Plymouth in 1621; and the Puritan settlement of Boston in the 1630s. Few would know that John Smith of Virginia fame actually explored the Massachusetts Bay area in 1614 after his Chesapeake adventures and coined the name "New England," or that the *Mayflower* was not the earliest ship to bring English settlers to New England, or that the land which would become Boston was neither the first nor the only destination of John Winthrop's Puritan fleet.

Several would-be colonizers brought ships to the New England coast before the Pilgrim landing. Captain Bartholomew Gosnold, for example, explored and named Cape Cod as well as Martha's Vineyard in 1602, found natives who had already traded with Europeans, but had to abandon his plans to leave settlers when it became clear that they lacked the provisions needed to survive.[20] In 1607 a settlement was planted at the mouth of the Kennebec River in Maine, only to be abandoned within a year. Between 1614 and 1620, Captain John Smith made several attempts to assemble and dispatch colonizing ships to New England but storms, pirates and the collapse of his sponsors' finances doomed his efforts. Meanwhile, large numbers of ships made the voyage from England to New England, but only for fishing and trade, not permanent colonization. Captain Richard Whitbourn reported seeing hundreds of fishing vessels on the New England coast in 1615 alone.[21] In addition to the English, fishermen from France, Spain, Portugal and Italy all tossed their nets in the rich North American waters.[22]

By 1620 the separatists who had fled England to Holland for religious reasons obtained leave from the South Virginia patent holders in London to settle in those lands. These self-described "Pilgrims" hoped to land the *Mayflower* near the mouth of the Hudson River, but instead made landfall at the tip of Cape Cod and eventually found a place inside the protective arm of Cape Cod which they called Plymouth.[23] The area had only recently been re-chartered as North Virginia to a group of west Englanders led by Sir Ferdinando Gorges, who was happy to give a patent to the Pilgrims for their Plymouth plantation. Once they survived their early, hard years, the Pilgrims began to explore the lands around them, including Cape Cod, Massachusetts Bay and Narragansett Bay, for fishing and for farming.

The fishing fleets of Weymouth, the thriving port city of Dorsetshire, had continued to exploit North American fishing grounds in the first decades of the seventeenth century. Thirty or more boats would make the several week trip across the Atlantic to the rich banks along and above New England, take cod by the thousands, dry and salt the fish, and carry them back to southern Europe to trade for wine, fruit and other goods favored at home in England. The Rev. John White of Dorchester took an interest in these Dorset men, knowing they would be away from their families "for up to nine months at a time without proper accommodation, fresh food or spiritual guidance."[24] Looking for ways to meet their needs, as well as to generate profits for investors, White led a group forming the Dorchester Company of Adventurers. In

1623 the company secured a patent for lands on the north coast of Massachusetts near Cape Ann where the necessary dry fishing stages and flakes as well as settlements could be located.[25]

By 1626 it was clear that the venture was failing, but dozens of settlers remained near Cape Ann at the new town of Salem to which they had moved. Rev. White and his partner John Humfry worked to keep the project alive, sending additional settlers, stores and a new governor in John Endicott in 1628. They reformed the company, obtained a new patent as the New England Company and reached out to "sundry gentlemen of influence"—potential new investors in London and Lincolnshire known to them through a combination of commercial and clerical networks.[26] Yet another patent was obtained by the newly expanded group, this one in the form of a royal charter for the Company of the Massachusetts Bay in New England in 1629, with boundaries that would be the subject of dispute and litigation for years. Planning began for a major resettlement from England to Massachusetts.

By this time there were already dozens of settlements along the coast of New England from Plymouth all the way north to Saco, with as many as 500 English planted in coastal communities. Some of the names remain on maps today (Weymouth, Braintree, Cape Ann), while others have been superseded (Naumkeag, Shawmut, Nantasket, Pemaquid) by more familiar ones (Salem, Boston, Portsmouth, Dover). Early English settlements appeared not only in New England but up and down the Atlantic coast of what would become the United States. Historian David Hackett Fischer has estimated that there were "more than thirty English-speaking settlements" established between 1578 and 1625.[27]

John Winthrop enters the story here. Concerned about the potential for interference by the King and his Archbishop in their plans for colonizing Massachusetts, the Puritan proprietors of the reorganized Company of the Massachusetts Bay decided that the new company would be governed from the colony and the charter would be taken on the ship rather than left in England.[28] Winthrop, though not the most prominent of the venturers, was a well-connected and skilled lawyer known to be trustworthy as well as sound in his Puritan faith. Moreover, unlike some of the other significant leaders of the enterprise, Winthrop was willing to make the permanent move to the new colony. He was elected Governor of the colony-to-be at a meeting in London on October 20, 1629. Plans began immediately for assembling a Puritan fleet to sail to New England in 1630 to build on the foundation of towns and settlers already established by the Dorchester group.

Some of Winthrop's friends and relatives tried to discourage him from abandoning his family manor and legal career for the hardship and uncertainty of the American wilderness. But he had thought carefully about making the move. Winthrop's most recent biographer, Francis J. Bremer, highlights several arguments presented by Winthrop in a document prepared for meetings of potential supporters. Winthrop saw God's judgment in the difficulties faced by Protestants in Europe, as well as the opportunity to make converts for the right version of the Gospel (the reformed Protestant version, not the Roman Catholicism being spread by the French Jesuits). He noted the growth of population in England and the impoverishment of many, as well as the corrupting effect of economic difficulties on business and professional men. He characterized the New World as "the Lord's garden" that should not be allowed "to lie waste without improvement." Economic opportunity was interwoven with religious duty by Winthrop, as it would consistently be in the new colony.[29]

The first four ships of what historians often call the "Winthrop Fleet," the *Arbella, Talbot, Ambrose* and *Jewel*, left port on March 29, 1630 and made landfall nine weeks later, on June 6. Rev. White's separate Dorset-based passengers on the *Mary & John* left earlier and had already arrived in the Bay area at the end of May. Other ships followed that year, a total of eleven vessels carrying 700 passengers (of whom some 200 died in the early years of the colony). The exodus would continue for much of the next ten years, as more than ten thousand English men and women crossed the Atlantic to New England between 1630 and 1640 to build new lives.[30]

After landing at Salem, where Endicott and others of the Dorchester Company had resettled, Winthrop and the first hundreds of immigrants spread out around the Charles and Mystic Rivers in search of suitable places for houses and farms. Charlestown, Mystic (later called Medford), Newtown (later Cambridge), Watertown, Roxbury and Dorchester were among the earliest settlements as the prominent men of the enterprise spread out and took their extended family and community groups with them. The Shawmut peninsula south of the Charles River provided both fresh spring water and a defensible location. The area had been inhabited for several years by one William Blaxton (also written Blackstone), who was part of an earlier attempt at colonization under Robert Gorges in 1623. At Blaxton's suggestion and after investigating the site, Governor Winthrop's group and a number of others removed from Charlestown to a settlement on the isthmus they called Boston (leaving disappointed the residents of both Charlestown and Newtown, who had hoped to have the governing authorities reside with them). The town was named in honor of the home of Isaac Johnson of Lincolnshire, one of the leaders of the colony who, along with his wife the Lady Arbella Johnson, died just months after their arrival.[31]

The bounds of Boston of 1630 looked very different from the land within the city limits today (indeed, the filling and reclamation of low lying areas over centuries has more than doubled the original landmass). The only access by land required crossing a narrow neck from the southwest onto the peninsula, which included a ridge line of hills and a plain running down to coves and marshes along its various waterfronts. The new settlers set about building shelters, which ranged from rude wigwams to plank houses, and planting crops. Blaxton sold 45 acres of level land to the colonists for use as a "common," an area large enough for pasturing the community's farm animals.

Rules of governance had been provided in the colony's charter, and so the first Great and General Court session was held in

Charlestown in August 1630. John Winthrop was re-elected as governor, an office he would hold for eleven of the next eighteen years, although not without disappointing losses in several elections as the colony navigated internal differences as well as external challenges and threats.

And a church was built, the First Church. One of those who had sailed to New England and moved to Boston with Winthrop was the Rev. John Wilson. Chosen to lead the church at Boston and Charlestown in August 1630, he served as the pastor of the First Church until his death in 1667. Rev. Wilson was an uncle of Edward Rawson (his mother Margaret's brother) and this family connection is very likely a principal reason for Rawson's emigration to Massachusetts in 1636.[32]

The ships continued to arrive. As one historian describes the years between 1630 and 1634: "[N]ear twenty considerable ships [arrived] every year, since the second... With such a number of passengers, that the inhabitants were forced to look out for new places of settlement, so, in these four years every desirable place fit for plantations on the sea-coast was taken up."[33] Some looked beyond the sea coast; one group settled at Concord, about twelve miles inland in one of the earliest examples of "westward migration" in America.

New places were needed to meet the need for farmland for the newcomers and grazing meadows for their livestock. But there was often more to the story. When the Rev. Thomas Hooker and a large group from Newtown petitioned the General Court in 1634 for leave to replant themselves in the Connecticut River valley, they explained that it was "a very fertill place... and well stored with meddow." It was also clear, however, that Hooker and his church were unhappy with the tight reins held by the Puritan leaders in Boston, for whom church and state bore little separation and expressions of religious differences could (and often did in ensuing years) lead to accusations of sedition.[34] Hooker, in particular, understood this; he had been hounded by Archbishop Laud while in England and fled reluctantly to Massachusetts.

The difficult issue of resettlement of his group to Connecticut was solved by the Court in the only practical way, by authorizing a move that likely would have occurred whether or not authorized. Although the move could weaken the Bay in the short term, it would expand trading opportunities and access to the Indian fur trade as well as challenge competing Dutch claims to the area. By the end of 1635, more than sixty settlers had crossed the wilderness to plant Hartford.[35] Other groups settled the Connecticut River valley in nearby Wethersfield (the site of an early Plymouth Colony trading post) and Windsor (initially led by Roger Ludlow and a disaffected group from Dorchester).

Lands at the mouth of the Connecticut River became the focus of a group of Londoners that included Lord Brooke and Lord Saye and Sel. They engaged Winthrop's son John Winthrop, Jr. to lead the effort as governor, and a military outpost was constructed on the coast in 1635. Ambitious plans to create an entirely new colonization model, based on large estates for the gentry and inheritance of titles, fell apart when the King demanded the right to require letters of passage approving who could emigrate and who could not. The outpost, however, remained and became the nucleus of Saybrook.[36]

The rapid expansion into the Connecticut coast and river valley inevitably and quickly put the English into conflict with the Pequot natives living there. Plymouth and Massachusetts had not faced serious threats from the indigenous tribes in eastern Massachusetts, as those lands had nearly been cleared of Indians by smallpox and other European diseases introduced by early traders.[37] John Winthrop made the observation in 1634, appalling to modern ears on a number of levels, that with the scourge of smallpox "the Lord hath cleared our title to what we possess."[38] But the southern coast of Connecticut and the interior remained populated by Narragansetts, Pequots, Mohegans, Mohawks and a number of other tribes. The Pequots, in particular, bridled as English traders and settlers poured into their lands.

A trader named John Stone from Virginia had been killed by natives on the Connecticut River in 1634. Soon after, the Pequots sought to engage the Bay Colony in an alliance to aid them against their tribal enemies. Colonial insistence on punishment of Stone's murderers, however, went unheeded and spiked tensions. Other killings followed, until the murder of another trader, Boston's John Oldham, on Block Island in 1636. After discussions with the Narragansetts, who pointed to the Pequots as responsible for the murder, Massachusetts troops were assembled and sent to Block Island to avenge the crime. Although assaulted with arrows as they landed, the colonists were unable to find and kill more than a handful of the attackers, so they burned native wigwams and destroyed cornfields. As they landed next on the mainland to pursue the Pequots, the scene of laying waste the land was repeated.

As Connecticut authorities feared would happen, the Pequots, led by their sachem Sassacus, chose to retaliate against them rather than against the Boston men. Saybrook was attacked in February 1637, and Wethersfield in April. Connecticut and Massachusetts agreed that war against the Pequots was the only answer. After Roger Williams helped to negotiate support from the powerful Narragansetts, the colonies in May 1637 assembled a combined force of 100 militia along with hundreds of Narragansett and dozens of Mohegans. They surrounded a Pequot fortified village near Mystic, assaulted and set it afire, and then massacred any who tried to escape the conflagration. The captains reported that 600–700 Indians (including many women and children) were killed in the attack, and another 100 or more natives died in subsequent skirmishes as the English proceeded back to the coast.

As the surviving Pequots, including their leaders Sassacus and Mononotto, scattered and fled to the west, a second colonial force was assembled in June 1637. They found, attacked and defeated a Pequot band, killing or enslaving dozens. They next assaulted Pequots hiding in a swamp near present day Fairfield, killing the men and taking prisoner many of the women and children. Mononotto was caught by the English and put to death. Meanwhile, Sassacus fell into the hands of the Mohawks, who executed him and sent his body parts to Boston to curry favor with the colony. As described by historian Bernard Bailyn, "[T]he

Pequots' threat had been eliminated in a genocidal slaughter." It would be forty years before another, much greater Indian danger would arise.[39]

Lands newly and brutally cleared of the Pequots provided prime opportunities for further English settlements. New Haven (1637), Guilford and Milford (both 1639) were organized from England, drawing hundreds of new settlers, and were followed by Stamford (1641), New London (1646) and many others. Rapid expansion was taking place in other areas as well. Early Rhode Island towns included Cumberland (1634), Providence (1636), Portsmouth (1638), Newport (1638) and Warwick (1642). Parts of Massachusetts that later became the royal colony of New Hampshire saw growth into Rye (1635), Exeter and Hampton (both 1638), in addition to existing towns in Portsmouth and Dover. Other new villages were planted in Maine (e.g., Wells in 1643) and on Long Island (e.g., Gravesend and Southampton in 1640).

Two driving forces stand out in explaining this rapid expansion: land hunger and religious quarrels. The authorities in Massachusetts had imposed a particular model for the planting of new towns, which included how land would be distributed and used. They also provided for a limit to the number of families that might settle within the confines of the new town and prohibited relocation to the town without permission of the town's leaders. New immigrants naturally looked to "empty" lands as soon as they could, as did existing settlers with growing families and expanding livestock herds.

Religion was the other great driver of relocation to new settlements. Having left England in no small part to protect their ability to worship and believe independently of the heavy hand of King, Archbishop and Church of England, the colonial authorities wielded their own heavy hand against religious nonconformists in the Bay Colony. Roger Williams, Ann Hutchinson and John Wheelwright were all banished for perceived errors in their religious views and for their failures to obey demands that they cease misleading their parishioners and disrupting the peace. Settlements in Rhode Island and Maine resulted when those three left and in each case took a number of adherents with them. At a more local level, when a group within a town's church became dissatisfied with the theology being preached, they would often leave to found a new church in a new town. Historian L.K. Mathews writes that "church quarrels were a most fruitful source of new towns in Massachusetts and Connecticut."[40]

Events in England wrote the next chapter in the New England story. The conflict between the Puritans in Parliament and King Charles continued to escalate in 1640, with the scales tipping toward Parliament. The Earl of Strafford, one of the King's favorites, was imprisoned, tried and then executed for treason. Archbishop Laud followed him to the confines of the Tower (and, in 1645, to the executioner's block). Civil war broke out in 1642 after the King's invasions of Scotland and later Ireland portended military suppression of Parliament. At the head of Parliament's "New Model Army," Puritans Thomas Fairfax and Oliver Cromwell defeated the royalists and, eventually, placed King Charles under house arrest and then outright imprisonment. When the King continued from confinement to plot a return to power, he was tried, condemned and executed in January 1649.[41]

The impact of this conflict on New England, beginning in 1640, was like the tightening of a spigot. Puritans in England focused on their battle at home rather than on faraway colonies. As they began to feel secure, with their royalist persecutors on the run, the Puritans no longer had need to flee across the Atlantic. Historian Samuel G. Drake reports that the ships full of new colonists stopped coming into the Bay in 1640 and that "emigration entirely ceased during the year." Bailyn goes further, saying not only did "the westward flow of desperate emigrants" dwindle and stop, but that "the upheaval in England inverted the migration pattern" as many chose to go home to join the Puritans in their fight or to regain the lands or parishes they had left behind.[42]

The colonial economy to that point relied heavily on the steadily increasing population provided by newly arriving immigrants as well as on the trans-Atlantic trade with England. Fewer newcomers meant lower demand for land and farm products, as well as lower prices and fewer markets for what the colonies could produce. The decade of the 1640s was a hard one, as the colonies struggled to reinvent their economy both through greater self-reliance (as, for example, in manufacturing) and through the expansion of trade with England's West Indies colonies (emphasizing the export of fish, timber, wood products like barrel staves, farm produce and livestock).[43]

These were the years in which Gillingham's Edward Rawson rose to prominence in the Colony. He became the Newbury town clerk in 1638 and was chosen as one of Newbury's representatives in the Colony's House of Deputies in 1639.[44] Recognized by his colleagues for his abilities, Rawson was named Secretary of the House of Deputies in 1646, and was then elected as Secretary of the Great and General Court of the Massachusetts Bay Colony in 1650 at the age of only 35. He and his wife Rachel moved from Newbury to Boston, their home not far from the Common on a street that would eventually be known as "Rawson's Lane."

By the time the English monarchy was restored in 1660 under King Charles II and the attention of London again turned to English colonies abroad, New England had found its footing and was enjoying its relative independence. An early delegation of agents for the colony to the new King succeeded in gaining confirmation of the colony's patent and charter, although the colony was also instructed to review its laws for consistency with the King's authority and to permit the use of the Church of England's Book of Common Prayer. Royal commissioners sent from London in 1664 to investigate and resolve certain disputes raised in allegations against Boston found the colonial authorities less than fully cooperative despite their renewed allegiance to the Crown.[45]

And the colonies continued to grow and to expand. Bailyn (*The Barbarous Years*, p. 514) estimates that even without the numbers of arriving immigrants in the first ten years, the population of New England was doubling every 27 years. The resulting demand for new lands and new towns to accommodate this growth pushed the frontier south, west and north through the

1650s and 1660s until, inevitably, something or someone pushed back. The push back was fierce when it came.

✻   ✻   ✻   ✻

Secretary Edward Rawson remained comfortable in his Boston home on Rawson's Lane while so many other colonists restlessly moved on. The town he moved into after leaving Newbury in 1650 had grown and changed year by year. Wharves extended from the major streets. Stonework batteries protected the city on its north and the south faces to the harbor. The colonists had begun to fill the marshy areas and to pave the main roads. A beacon stood at the top of the tallest of the three hills of the Tramont. Handsome multi-story brick or stone houses replaced lower, plank structures in many parts of town, and impressive churches were built by congregations new and old. Gardens and orchards graced the land, even as much of the farming moved to the mainland west of the isthmus. As historian Bailyn describes, the Pilgrim merchants of Boston "sought to recreate the life they had known at home... The settling together of friends and the use of old street names were fragments of the settlers' never-ending attempts to make the wilderness of America familiarly English."[46]

As the colony's secretary, Rawson had a hand in (or put his signature on documents related to) many of the critical issues faced by the colony during his thirty-six years of service: sometimes fraught relations with the authorities back in England; Indian wars; religious disputes and persecution of the Quakers; some of the early witch trials; the new King's pursuit of the accused regicides of his father Charles I; and, of course, the expansion of settlers into new towns. He also served as the colony's agent in providing supplies to the natives in the area. His Boston had grown into a thriving town of 7,000 residents by 1690.[47]

Rawson's long tenure as Secretary of the General Court ended in 1686 after the Crown's reorganization of the colonies into the Dominion of New England and the appointment of the royal governor Sir Edmund Andros, who purged the government of its former leaders. (Andros was himself ousted by the colonists in the Boston uprising of 1689 following the accession of King William and Queen Mary.) Before his death in 1693, now former Secretary Rawson could reflect with satisfaction on what he had accomplished in nearly sixty years as a New Englander and on the legacy he left for his family. Three sons had returned to England, as had his tragedy-befallen daughter, Rebecca.[48] Another son, William, a successful Boston merchant, settled on the Braintree farm he purchased from the heirs of his great-uncle the Rev. John Wilson. But the Secretary's youngest son, the Harvard-educated Rev. Grindal Rawson, accepted the call and the challenge of moving to the frontier town of Mendon, Massachusetts in 1680. When two of William's sons followed their Uncle Grindal and migrated to Mendon as well, a new chapter in the Rawson story began.[49]

---

[1] The dismantling of the royal forest in favor of revenue-generating estates or leaseholds and the widespread uprising that resulted is a fascinating episode that lies beyond the scope of this narrative. It did, however, apparently touch the lives of Rawson relatives. Rachel (Perne) Rawson's parents Richard and Rachel Perne were tenant farmers leasing a mansion house called East Haimes near the forest boundary. When rioters in 1643 took advantage of the lawless environment created by the English Civil War to destroy fences and fill ditches, a group of ruffians confronted Rachel Perne, threatening her and lighting fires on the property until paid a ransom to depart. Her father (Richard Greene, the grandfather of Edward Rawson's wife Rachel) apparently served as agent for the king's principal leaseholder and reported to him that "the land is all thrown abroad" by the violence. *See* John Porter, *Gillingham's Royal Forest*, pp. 75–76 and 87. Edward and Rachel Rawson were long since settled in Massachusetts by this time.

[2] *See* Boorstin, *Discoverers*, pp. 142–43, 155, 228; Beer, *Origins*, pp. 2–3.

[3] As described by Samuel Eliot Morison, "America was discovered accidentally by a great seaman who was looking for something else; when discovered it was not wanted; and most of the exploration for the next fifty years was done in the hope of getting through or around it." Morison, *American People*, p. 23.

[4] Dwyer, p. 69.

[5] Morison, *American People*, p. 40; *European Discovery*, pp. 440–41, 510–66, 568–78, 587–605..

[6] Morison, *European Discovery*, p. 558.

[7] Beer, pp. 26–35.

[8] Morison, *European Discovery*, pp. 618, 640.

[9] Morison, *European Discovery*, p. 574.

[10] This contrasts with the "wet" curing technique of the French and Spanish fishermen, who filled their barrels with cod and salt before heading for home. Morison, *European Discovery*, p. 476.

[11] According to Bailyn, the population in England grew from 4.1 million in 1600 to 5.3 million in 1650. *The Barbarous Years*, p. 165.

[12] Ackroyd, *Rebellion*, p. 154.

[13] Bailyn, *The Barbarous Years*, p. 378.

[14] The "disafforestation" of the royal forest in Gillingham and the withdrawal of grazing rights from forest lands caused a number of affected locals to burn down hedges, destroy new fences, fill in ditches and threaten the landlord's workmen. Disturbances began in 1626, but spiked again in 1643 and 1645 as the English Civil War deprived the area of consistent law enforcement and protection. *See* Porter, at pp. 39, 74 et seq.

[15] *See*, e.g., Roger Daniels, *Coming to America*, p. 17.

[16] Some historians, however, have concluded that the narrative of widespread persecution against the Puritans led by an Anglican version of Torquemada, Archbishop Laud, as the primary driver of emigration was a revisionist construct by the Rev. Cotton Mather and other later writers. *See* Daniels, p. 43, in contrast with Fischer, *Albion's Seed*, p. 16.

[17] Historian Roger Daniels writes that "of one hundred and ninety-eight known voyages to New England in the 1630s, only one resulted in shipwreck, and even then not all were drowned." *Coming to America*, p. 49; see also Fischer, p. 17 n. 8. Many passengers, however, sickened and died from scurvy, smallpox or other diseases.

[18] *See*, e.g., Fischer and Kelly, p. 18 ("The joint-stock company was

a powerful engine for the mobilization of energy and capital.")

[19] *See*, e.g., Bremer, *John Winthrop*, at pp. 164–65.

[20] Drake, pp. 12–14; Kelso, *Jamestown*, p. 120. Bartholomew Gosnold would die in Jamestown, Virginia in 1607, one of many casualties to attacks by Virginia Indians. He has been described as "the overlooked principal figure in the planting of the Virginia colony." Kelso, p. 138.

[21] Drake, pp. 22–25.

[22] Mann, p. 54.

[23] Morison, *American People*, p. 55.

[24] Dwyer, *Dorset Pioneers*, pp. 27, 70.

[25] The Dorchester group's right to the Cape Ann area was disputed by the Plymouth Colony, which also made use of the area for shore support of its fishermen. A peaceful resolution was achieved, and a large marker embedded in a stony cliff still marks the event in these words: "On this site in 1623 a company of fishermen and farmers from Dorchester England under the direction of Rev. John White founded the Massachusetts Bay Colony. From that time the fisheries, the oldest industry in the Commonwealth, have been uninterruptedly pursued from this port. Here in 1628 Gov. Roger Conant by wise diplomacy averted bloodshed between contending factions one led by Myles Standish of Plymouth the other by Capt. Hawes, a notable exemplification of arbitration in the beginnings of New England."

[26] Ebenezer Clapp Jr., *History of the Town of Dorchester, Massachusetts*, pp. 14–16.

[27] Fischer and Kelly, p. 13, citing Fischer, *Albion's Seed*, p. 184.

[28] Jumping forward to highlight a historical coincidence, when King Charles II in 1665 demanded that the colony's proprietors produce the charter, it was Secretary Edward Rawson who was directed by the General Court to bring the document out of the archives to be held by a small committee of deputies pending a response to the King's demand.

[29] Bremer, pp. 157–58.

[30] The ten thousand or more souls of the Great Puritan Migration were themselves only a part of a much broader movement to the west during the seventeenth century. One prominent historian estimates that 400,000 people left Britain for the Americas by 1700. Bailyn, *The Barbarous Years*, p. 366.

[31] Drake, pp. 92–97.

[32] In the 1630s Wilson found himself among those criticized and caught up in the "Antinomian Controversy" in which Ann Hutchinson was tried, convicted and banished. Hutchinson and others preached a gospel of salvation by grace without regard to behavior, which her opponents characterized as antinomian, heretical and dangerous. Hutchinson became the Cassandra of the Bay Colony, warning of the coming of God's wrath at the authorities.

[33] Drake, p. 170.

[34] To cite just one illustration, from Drake's *Antiquities* (p. 252): "One Hugh Bewett was banished for maintaining that he was free from original sin, and that true Christians could live without committing any sin. By the order of the Court, he was to be gone in fifteen days upon pain of death, and if he returned he should be hanged."

[35] Drake, pp. 173–177.

[36] Bremer, p. 260.

[37] Historical estimates of the native mortality rate from diseases carried into New England by European traders and settlers range as high as 75 to 90%. *See*, e.g., Calloway, *Western Abenakis of Vermont, 1600–1800*, pp. 37–39.

[38] Daniels, p. 7.

[39] *See* Bailyn, *The Barbarous Years*, pp. 444–449; Drake, pp. 198–216; Bremer, pp. 262–271; Matthews, pp. 23–24.

[40] The Puritans found much to quarrel about in their religious views. Accusative labels such as "antinomian" and "familist" were applied to those whose perspective on salvation, justification or sanctification (among many other sources of dispute) did not comport with the majority's line. Even eminent divines like the Rev. John Cotton were accused and tried for teaching that which was thought to stray too far from Puritan orthodoxy. In 1654, the General Court ordered that no man could serve as a Deputy who "was not correct in the main doctrines of religion." Drake, p. 337.

[41] *See* generally Ackroyd, pp. 244–310.

[42] Bailyn, p. 470; Drake, p. 249; Bremer, p. 329. Bailyn estimates (*The Barbarous Years*, p. 473) that between 7% and 12% of immigrants returned to England between 1640 and 1650, and perhaps as many as one-third of the clerics who had come to America went back home.

[43] Bailyn, pp. 477–490.

[44] Coffin, *History of Newbury*, p. 46; *Rawson Family Memorial*, pp. 3–4.

[45] Drake, pp. 360–361.

[46] From Bailyn, *The New England Merchants in the Seventeenth Century*, quoted by Walter Muir Whitehill in *Boston: A Topographical History*, at pp. 12–13.

[47] Whitehill, p. 37.

[48] Rebecca Rawson married a man whose false claim to be the son of prominent English jurist Lord Chief Justice Hale—"Lord Thomas Hale," as the suitor styled himself —was believed by her family and the Boston community at large. She returned to England with him, only to be abandoned at their ship's landing by the husband she learned too late was a fraud and bigamist named Thomas Rumsey. When she tried to return to New England after several years, Rebecca Rawson perished when her ship was swallowed up by an earthquake in the Jamaica harbor of Port Royal. *See New England Journal of History*, Vol. 56 No. 1, Fall 1999.

[49] *See generally* Appendix One.

II.
SOUTHWEST IN MASSACHUSETTS: BOSTON TO MENDON

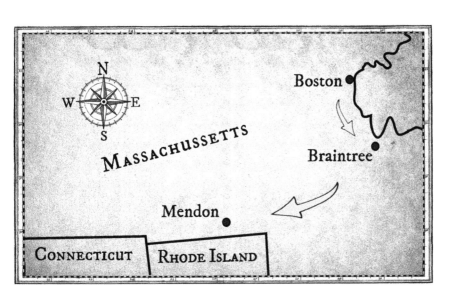

The devastation must have shocked the men, even though they had known what to expect. Now that the Indian uprising called King Philip's War had ended, the settlers of Mendon, Massachusetts were anxious to return to the place they'd been forced to abandon. Before the war, back in the optimistic years between 1667 and 1675, they had with great care built homes and meeting houses and mills. They had worked tirelessly to clear the forest and cultivate fields, to carve roads and construct bridges. They had recruited dozens of families from among their neighbors back in Weymouth and Braintree to join them in their exciting enterprise -- creating a new home far away from the increasingly crowded coast. And now this.

Soot-blackened stone foundations were all that remained of the houses they'd fled, all burned to the ground. The largest pile marked the site of the meeting house where they'd thanked the Lord for their many blessings. The mills had fallen into the river, the bridges mostly collapsed, the roads and fields reclaimed by the forest the settlers had been so bold as to think they could hold back. The bleached bones of some of their livestock lay scattered among the ruins. The men had talked as they rode the two days from Boston about what they might expect to find here, some more hopeful than others. But tears now rolled down the faces of even the hardest of the men. One pointed out the spot where the wife and son of their friend Matthias Puffer had been killed in the first attack in 1675.

Oaths were sworn. *We'll rebuild Mendon, with God's help. The land is still ours, and much safer now than it was before the war. We did it once, we can do it again.*

By 1660, when a king sat once more on the throne of England, the Great and General Court of the Massachusetts Bay Colony had developed and implemented a well-understood process for those who wished to start a new settlement. As explained by historian Samuel Eliot Morison: "When members of a village community felt crowded for space, they petitioned the colonial assembly for a new township. A committee was appointed to satisfy Indian claimants, to settle on a village site and lay out lots. Home lots and space for the meetinghouse, which served both as church and town hall, were laid out around a village green, with a surrounding belt of planting lots for growing crops."[1]

The distribution of lots measuring five to ten acres each might be done by a lottery. Some of the land would be held in common (e.g., a village green or community garden); other land would be held back for future distribution to new settlers. The object, as described by migration historian Frederick Merk, was to create a "community of small landholders." The new settlement would often (though not always) be adjacent to an existing town; among other benefits, this principle of "compactness of settlements" could provide for preserving common cultural values; limit speculation in lands; permit settlers to control the arrival of outsiders; and facilitate common defense against natives.[2]

Bernard Bailyn adds that the group might be secular or it might be led by an ecclesiastical, depending on the reasons for the relocation. He also points out that plans needed to include such essentials as roads and bridges that might be needed. The specifics of awarding lottery shares or particular lots to individuals for their farms and grazing meadows often varied based on such factors as the prominence and resources of the leading families as well as the form of land use experienced by the dominant group of settlers in their native counties of England (for example, as Bailyn explains, whether they hailed from the West Country with its model of open field agriculture or from East Anglia where private and fenced holdings were the norm).[3]

This was the process used by the Weymouth and Braintree

families who first settled Mendon, thirty miles southwest of Boston. The General Court in May of 1659 took action on the petition of a group of prospective settlers, granting them "liberty to seek out a place." In May of 1660, the Court approved their petition to form a new plantation, and a few months later issued an order creating a committee to conduct the process for settling the chosen location. After identifying the natives who claimed possession of the lands, the committee oversaw the negotiation of the sale of the land for a payment of 24 pounds. A prominent colonist without a financial interest in the transaction, John Eliot (who is often referred to as the "Apostle to the Indians") served as one of the witnesses to the deed. By 1662, the committee had worked with the petitioners to draw up a set of rules of governance for the new plantation. These included such matters as the size of lots; regulations for sales of lots; the approval of new inhabitants; and the selection and settling of a minister.[4]

The first settler families arrived in 1663: George Aldrich, John Harber, Daniel Lovett, John Moore, Matthias Puffer, Ferdinando Thayer, and John Woodland. They were soon followed by Joseph Aldridge, Walter Cook, John Gwiney, John Jepson, John Rockett, Abraham Staples, John Thompson and Joseph White.[5]

In May of 1667, almost exactly eight years after the first petition, the General Court gave the new plantation the name Mendon (previously referred to as "Squinshepauke") and granted it "Towne Privileges as other Townes of this jurisdiction do enjoy." Secretary Rawson provided his attestation and signature to the Court's order.[6]

The citizens of Mendon quickly got down to business. At a town meeting in June, 1667, a council of selectman was chosen. They, in turn, appointed the first town officers: a "Fence Viewer" (empowered to order the building and maintenance of fences to protect crops from farm animals) and a "Hog Reive" (who could require that hogs be kept restrained, again to protect crops). Over the next few years, the council approved the construction of a meeting house, the calling of a minister (the Rev. Joseph Emerson, an

ancestor of Ralph Waldo Emerson), the construction of saw pits
and corn mills and even the establishment of 20 shilling bounties
for the killing of the wolves that threatened the settlers' livestock.[7]

By 1675 there were 38 families settled in Mendon, most
engaged in farming their land and keeping livestock. As they
carefully tended their fields early that summer, the Mendon settlers had no idea that these crops would never be harvested. Their
proud new settlement would instead very soon be at the center of
a bloody war that would threaten all of New England.

Relations between the native peoples and the English settlers had always been more complex and more fraught with tensions than the simplistic, Thanksgiving versions of history let
on. Behind the persisting Thanksgiving image of the benevo-
lent Pokomakets Massasoit and Squanto bringing food and
solace to the desperate Plymouth pilgrims in 1621, the natives
of sixteenth and seventeenth century Massachusetts and surrounding areas were a bewildering patchwork of Wampanoags
and Narragensetts, of Nipmucs and Abenakis, of Mohegans and
Mahicans and Pequots. Each grouping identified itself with lands
which shared loose boundaries. Each tribe had reasons to ally
itself with others at times, and to fight their erstwhile allies at
other times. At a larger level, all of these Algonquian language
tribes lived in conflict with the Mohawks and other Iroquois
tribes who lived to the west of the Connecticut River. This was no
monolithic Indian nation.

The Europeans landing on their shores, of course, presented the many native tribes with their own confusing can-
vas of Frenchman to the north, Spaniards to the south, Dutch
and Swedes and English in the middle. Nor were Bradford and
Brewster and the rest of the *Mayflower* passengers anywhere near
the first to come from Europe to these parts. From Nova Scotia
to the Chesapeake, coastal villages and seasonal settlements had
cropped up wherever needed by fisherman and by fur traders.
Scores of such outposts were in place by the turn of the seventeenth century, long before any Pilgrims or Puritans set foot in
Massachusetts.[8]

Historians have identified several key factors in the deteriorating relations between the natives and the English settlers in the decades prior to what has come to be known as "King Philip's War." Diseases brought from Europe had devastated native populations, which lacked immunities to smallpox and other maladies. The tribes had become reliant on trading with the English, particularly the fur trade, but were left vulnerable to changes in fashion in European capitals as beaver pelts were no longer coveted. The introduction of alcohol disrupted native village and family life, and the English ministers who sought to spread the Christian gospel further disrupted the native ways of living.[9] But the most significant factor, as explained by historians Eric B. Schultz and Michael J. Tougias, was the burgeoning English population and the increasing demand for the land the natives occupied: "The colonists increasingly sought not what the Narragansett (and other native peoples) could provide from the land, but the land itself. This radical shift in what had once been a cooperative relationship, more than any other single factor, would eventually lead them to war."[10]

The Pokamaket tribe of the Wampanoags had its own complicated and sometimes troubled history with the English. The great sachem Massasoit had stood with his translator and intermediary Squanto in aiding the Plymouth settlers in the first harsh years of the colony. As the English became more and more of an established fact of life for the Wampanoags, the sachem's sons had taken English names in 1660 to enable them to deal more effectively with the colonists, who were obviously not going away. Wamsutta, now called Alexander, succeeded his father on Massasoit's death, aided by his brother Metacom, known as Philip.

The English in Boston and in Plymouth tried to monitor activities of the natives that might prove threatening, often using the converted or "praying Indians" for this purpose. When concerns arose in 1662 that Alexander was aiding former colonists cast out by the Plymouth authorities, he was summoned and escorted to Plymouth and then to Boston to explain his actions. Something happened along the way, as Alexander took ill and soon died. Philip, the new sachem, suspected that his brother had been poisoned although the English insisted the death was from natural causes.[11]

Tensions continued to escalate as more of the English settled in the area and their unfenced livestock encroached on native hunting grounds.[12] When the colonists suspected Philip might be planning an attack on their villages in 1671, he was confronted and questioned. Backing away from whatever plans might have been afoot, he committed the Pokamaket to continued peaceful relations. But the 1675 murder of John Sassamon, a Harvard-educated praying Indian who maintained close ties to the English and who may have been suspected by the natives of informing the colonial authorities of plans for an attack, outraged the English even as the arrest, trial and execution of the three Pokamakets accused of the crime inflamed the tribe.[13]

The final spark was struck in the Plymouth Colony at Swansea two weeks later, in June of 1675. Skirmishes between settlers and natives had created an atmosphere of heightened tension. When one of the Pokamakets was spotted near a house in the settlement, he was shot and killed as he tried to run away. "King" Philip (as he came to be called by history) and his tribesmen soon retaliated by attacking Swansea and killing several of the English. The colonists raised their militia to pursue Philip, whose warriors quickly began to attack other settlements around the Narragansett Bay area. He then escaped to the west to hide among his allies the Nipmucs. Soon the Pokamakets were joined in a widespread rising against the English by the Nipmucs and the Narragansetts.[14]

The fledgling plantation at Mendon sat squarely within Nipmuc lands inside the borders of the Massachusetts Bay Colony. On July 19, 1675, a band of Nipmucs led by their sachem, Matoonas, attacked the Mendon farms and killed up to half a dozen settlers. No details have survived as to precisely how many of the English died. What is known is that the rest of the settlers quickly abandoned the village and fled back toward Boston. The Nipmucs then torched the vacated houses, barns, mills and the meeting house built by the settlers in 1668, burning everything to the ground.[15]

With the raid on Mendon, the war had spread from Plymouth to Massachusetts. Soon it reached all the way to the Connecticut River valley, as Deerfield and Springfield were attacked.[16] Colonial militias fared poorly in attempts to prevent or to punish the hit-and-run native attacks, as more than half of all English settlements in New England were struck. A major battle back near Narragansett Bay in December, now known as the "Great Swamp Fight," left more than 600 natives and 80 English dead but brought the war no closer to an end. Renowned historian Samuel Eliot Morison described this as "the toughest battle, not excepting Bunker Hill, ever fought on New England soil."[17] Others have described it as a terrible massacre of the natives by the colonial militias. As the snow melted in early 1676 and campaigns resumed, Indians raided close to Boston at Weymouth, Billerica and Braintree as well as at large settlements in Connecticut and Rhode Island.[18] Fifty-two towns were attacked, twelve of them (including Mendon) completely destroyed.

It was not until the summer of 1676 that events began to turn against the rebellious natives, with a relentless campaign by the colonial militia and the tribes aligned with them to capture or kill Philip. The increasingly isolated leader fled west again, leaving his wife and young son to be captured and sold into slavery in the West Indies. Philip's ally Matoonas surrendered with his Nipmuc tribesman, was transported to Boston and shot dead for his part in attacking Mendon and other towns.[19]

Finally, having lost many of his men in a battle with the Mohawk allies of the colonists, King Philip was himself tracked, ambushed and killed by natives working with the English. Reports exist that Philip's head was placed on a pike in Plymouth where it could still be seen twenty years later. Skirmishes continued into 1678, especially with the Abenakis in the north, but for much of New England the danger abated with the death of Philip.[20]

Many in the colonies had attributed their suffering at the hands of the Indians to a wrathful God.[21] Now seeing divine providence in the momentum that had turned their way, colonial authorities on June 20, 1676 issued a formal proclamation designating a "day of Solemn Thanksgiving and praise to God for such his Goodness and Favour" and for "reserving many of our Towns from Desolation Threatened, and attempted by the Enemy." Acknowledging that God had been sorely displeased but had now remembered mercy, the Court directed Secretary Rawson to issue this first official Thanksgiving proclamation.[22]

Scholars see a significance to King Philip's War that often goes unrecognized even by students of American history. The scope of human carnage as a percentage of population, with estimates ranging from 600 to nearly a thousand colonial deaths and perhaps three thousand among the natives, was "nearly twice that of the Civil War and more than seven times that of World War II."[23] The colonists were forced to learn new ways of fighting, what Puritan minister John Eliot termed "the skulking way of war," in order to meet the challenge; the lesson would prove useful in the coming episodes of the French and Indian War as well as in the American Revolution a century later.[24] They were also compelled to cooperate more closely with each other for the common defense of colonial settlements.

King Philip's War has been described as both an Indian Revolutionary War against the increasingly dominant English colonials as well as an Indian Civil War in which tribe fought against tribe, representing not only the traditional enmity of Iroquois against Algonquin but also pitting Algonquin against Algonquin.[25] Perhaps most significantly, the war in many ways set the pattern for the next two hundred years of conflict between relentlessly expanding European or later American settlements, and encroached, embattled and hunted natives.

Slowly at first, then more quickly, the English moved to rebuild destroyed settlements and to expand into abandoned or unprotected native lands. Mendon, as an example, was reoccupied by many of its founding families within two years of the end of the war in that area. Twenty families were settled there by 1680, including pre-war residents like Albee, Aldrich, Cook, Lovett,

Puffer, Rockett, Staples, Thayer and Thompson, as well as new names including Samuel Hayward, William Holbrook, Simon Peck, Samuel Read, John Sprague and Joe and Hope Tyler.[26] But the owners of nearly half of the land in Mendon never returned.[27]

Another significant newcomer moved to Mendon in 1680: the Rev. Grindal Rawson. One of two sons of Secretary Rawson who chose to remain in Massachusetts rather than return to England, Grindal Rawson graduated from Harvard in 1678 along with the prominent divine Rev. Cotton Mather and became qualified to preach the Gospel. Rawson was called to Mendon in 1680 and became the second "settled" minister there, serving until his death thirty-five years later. He married his second cousin Susanna Wilson of Medfield and they took seriously the scriptural mandate to be fruitful and multiply their numbers. Many of their children and grandchildren settled in Mendon and the surrounding area, while some began other lines of migrating Rawsons in Rhode Island, Connecticut, New York and Nova Scotia.

Upon Grindal Rawson's death in 1715, he was eulogized by his friend and classmate Mather "for his industrious oversight of the Flock in the wilderness," for his "intellectual abilities" (Rawson was often consulted by the General Court on ecclesiastical issues), and for "his doing the work of an Evangelist among our Indians" (Rawson mastered the local native dialect and authored a "Confession of Faith" in the native tongue).[28]

During Rev. Grindal Rawson's ministry in Mendon, in 1685, his father Secretary Edward Rawson was granted 2000 acres of land there by the General Court; he cleared title to the land with natives Thomas and Abigail Awassamoag. This land would later be described as "The Farm" and some part of it would be among the acreage separated from Mendon in 1719 to become the town of Bellingham.[29] Before Secretary Rawson's death in 1693 he gave his son, William (Grindal's older brother), 800 acres[30] of this land, setting the stage for two of William's sons (Grindal's nephews William and Nathaniel) to move to Mendon, pulled by economic opportunity and the connection with their well-established uncle and his family there.

King Philip's was neither the first nor the only war to afflict a growing population of New England in the seventeenth and eighteenth centuries. As will be described in detail later, nearly half of the seventy five years between 1688 and 1763 found the English colonists in North America enmeshed in war -- the westernmost theater of European great power wars on land and sea. England and France, Prussia and Spain, Austria and Russia, variously led by Hanovers and Hapsburgs and Bourbons, fought over succession to thrones, over competing territorial claims, and over trade and trade routes of the West Indies and the East Indies. Each stage of these European wars had a counterpart conflict in North America: the War of the League of Augsburg (1688-1697) was mirrored in the west by King William's War; the War of the Spanish Succession (1702-1713) by Queen Anne's War; the War of the Austrian Succession (1740-1748) by King George's War; and the Seven Years War (1754-1761) by what came to be called the French and Indian War[31] in North America.

The struggling settlers living on the frontier of England's North American colonies paid a steep price in these counterpart wars. In 1699, the General Court designated fourteen settlements as "frontier towns" which would receive military aid if attacked by Indians. Mendon was one of the towns designated. Deerfield, which would be the victim of a devastating raid in 1704, was another. Although Mendon was not attacked again directly during these troubled years, the wars certainly took a toll on its military age men. Mendon men responded to requests for militia during the French and Indian War; 41 men served in the expedition to Ticonderoga and Crown Point in 1759.[32] Others were involved in the attempt to relieve Fort William Henry on Lake George in 1757 and in the march on Montreal in 1760.

It was not only warfare that roiled the Massachusetts countryside, however. Mendon was one of many places caught up in the religious enthusiasm of the Great Awakening led in New England by Jonathan Edwards and George Whitefield beginning in the 1730s. Divisions of congregations into "New Lights" and "Old Lights" created controversy, split churches and even led some congregants to leave for new settlements where their theological views were shared. New Lights embraced the vision of personal salvation preached by the Great Awakening evangelists while Old Lights, wary of all this democratic enthusiasm, held more firmly to the traditional covenant. Mendon's established pastor, Rev. Joseph Dorr, aligned himself with the New Lights; he became the first moderator of the "Mendon Association" of New Light churches in the region in 1751 when the group was organized.[33]

The Rawsons continued to deepen their roots in the Mendon area throughout the eighteenth century. Rev. Dorr's wife Mary was a daughter of Rev. Grindal Rawson. Six of Grindal's eight children who survived to adulthood stayed in or around Mendon, as did many of their children. Grindal's nephews Nathaniel and William also moved from Braintree, where their father William and most of their other siblings had remained, to Mendon. Both played important civic roles there. Nathaniel was named a selectman, assessor and a committee member for the building of a new church in Mendon. His brother William, seven years older and a Harvard College graduate, served as a selectman, as town clerk and as school keeper at different times. Continuing a confusing Rawson family naming pattern into the next generation, William's son was also named William, the third consecutive use of the name. This William spent his entire life in Mendon; he was a lawyer who acted as town treasurer and town clerk for Mendon. In the next generation, the latter Williams's son Edward (again) was a farmer and a farrier who remained in Mendon and served in the Revolutionary War.

The Revolution began in Massachusetts but New England was not a primary theater of military action after the Minutemen's "shot heard round the world" in Lexington and Concord in 1775 and after the abandonment of Boston by the British under the threat of Washington's cannons on Dorchester Heights several months later. The men of Mendon responded to their neighbors' call for help as they had in prior wars, as 164 men marched off to Lexington after hearing the news of the skirmishes there and in

Concord. Mendon was also well represented in the Massachusetts Committee of Correspondence by Deacon Edward Rawson (a grandson of Rev. Grindal Rawson) and by Joseph Dorr (a son of Grindal's successor in the pulpit, Rev. Joseph Dorr, and also a grandson of Grindal's).[34]

In the years following the end of the Revolution, an economic depression hit much of the new United States, including Massachusetts. Back country farmers, whose only assets were in land and livestock, were hit particularly hard as currency lost value. Some states acted to provide relief to debtors but Massachusetts, which had recently raised land taxes and had a legislature full of men of propertied interests, refused. Enforcement of debts and foreclosures of mortgages in the courts created pressure that ignited mobs of debtors.

Beginning in the summer of 1786, Revolutionary War veteran Captain Daniel Shays led a fast growing armed mob in Massachusetts who sought to close the courts to protect debtors and mortgage holders. As the crowd swelled, Shays eventually moved against the courthouse and the arsenal in Springfield in January of 1787. National leaders, including George Washington, feared that the anarchy would metastasize: "Commotions of this sort, like snowballs, gather strength as they roll, if there is no opposition in the way to divide and crumble them." In a letter to Henry Knox, Washington described it as an important moment, when "anarchy & confusion" must not be allowed to prevail. The militia was called out, including 60 men from Mendon (the town was proud that none of its citizens had joined the rebellion).[35] The ensuing confrontation in Springfield left several rioters dead, but it was not until four thousand armed militia men showed up the next day under General Benjamin Lincoln that the mob was scattered and Shays's Rebellion ended.[36]

The economy of central Massachusetts regained its footing in the 1790s. Mendon found itself the focus of immigration from Rhode Island, and mills on the town's rivers, especially the Blackstone, powered a growing industrial base. Agriculture remained important, but was no longer the only engine of the local economy.[37] And with an increasingly limited amount of new land to be cultivated, Mendon may not have remained as attractive for farming as the country now being settled to the north and west. As observed by historian L.K. Mathews, "Over and over again the search for cheap and fertile land has been most potent, for until after the Revolution the chief business of all the colonial inhabitants save those in the coast towns was connected in some way with agriculture. When the best land ... had been taken, it became necessary to remove to some more productive region, or else to change one's occupation -- a thing not so easy of accomplishment" in those days.[38]

For many years, Mendon saw growth in its population as people increasingly moved from the Bay area into central Massachusetts and beyond. From the fifteen families who first settled Mendon in 1667 (and after the post-war resettlement by 1680), Mendon grew to 336 families in 1764 with a total of 1843 people. At the next accounting ten years later, the number of residents increased to 2322. The population of Mendon would reach a peak of 3524 in 1840 before it began to diminish.[39] Part of the reason for its reduced numbers was the repeated separation of parts of Mendon into new towns. Modern Mendon calls itself the "Mother of Municipalities" because eight separate towns have been created over the years from Mendon's original 64 square miles, usually at the behest of resident groups and over the objections of Mendon officials. These "daughter towns" are: Bellingham (created in 1719); Uxbridge (1727); Upton (1735); Northbridge (1772); Milford (1780); Blackstone (1845); Hopedale (1886); and Millville (1916).

Equally important, however, was the migration out of Mendon. Many farmers in central Massachusetts towns like Mendon found themselves attracted to the lands in the north, once those lands were no longer a highway for raiding parties and invading armies.

✱ ✱ ✱ ✱

Revolutionary War veteran Edward Rawson, part of the third consecutive generation of Rawsons in Mendon, stayed at home, and so did three of his brothers.[40] In the next generation, however, no fewer than nine Rawsons made their way up from Mendon to towns like Townshend, Jamaica, Wardsboro and Dover, all close together in the southwest corner of Vermont. To this day a village within the township of Jamaica, Vermont is known as Rawsonville,[41] named for another Revolutionary War veteran, Bailey Rawson. The pull factor of economic opportunity combined with the connection factor of family to create a common migration route north for these Rawsons and many others.[42]

Among the seven sons and daughters of Mendon's Edward Rawson, five remained in or close to Mendon just as their parents had. Another moved to nearby Rhode Island. But one sibling, Leonard, a single man of marriageable age skilled in farming and carpentry, decided in 1800 to follow the northwesterly path several of his first cousins had chosen. There is no way to know whether and what news from Leonard's Vermont cousins may have influenced his choice to leave his Mendon home. What is known is that Leonard picked up and moved to Pittsford, a Vermont town not very far north of the area in which those cousins had resettled.

How is it that Vermont, for so long a howling wilderness rightfully feared by Massachusetts settlers to its south, became a destination sought out by so many? Wars, as will be seen, begin that part of the tale.

---

[1] Morison, *American People*, p. 70.

[2] Merk, p. 34-36.

[3] Bailyn, pp. 419-428.

[4] *Mendon, Massachusetts 1667-1967*, pp. 25-27.

[5] Id., p. 29. Among these named first settlers, both Ferdinando Thayer and Walter Cook are direct ancestors of the author.

[6] Id.

[7] Id., p. 31-33.

[8] Schultz & Tougias, *King Philip's War*, p. 15.

[9] Id., pp. 15, 20.

[10] Id., p. 15; *see also* Merk, p. 40; Morison, *American People*, p. 108.

[11] Schultz & Tougias, pp. 23-24.

[12] Taylor, *American Colonies*, p. 47.

[13] Schultz & Tougias, pp. 24-29; Taylor, pp. 199-200; Morison, *American People*, p. 108. The meaning of the death of John Sassamon and subsequent events is explored by historian Jill Lepore, *The Name of War*, pp. 21-26.

[14] Schultz & Tougias, pp. 2, 42-43, 45-46.

[15] Id., pp. 44, 46.

[16] Id., pp. 50-51.

[17] Morison, *American People*, p. 110.

[18] Taylor, p. 200; Schultz & Tougias, pp. 53-55, 57, 60; Morison, *American People*, p. 110.

[19] Schultz & Tougias, pp. 66, 183-84.

[20] Schultz & Tougias, pp. 5, 68-69, 72; Morison, *American People*, p. 111.

[21] Taylor, p. 202; Morison, *American People*, p.107.

[22] University of Groningen, www.let.rug.nl.

[23] Schultz & Tougias, pp. 4-5; Taylor, p. 202; Philbrick, *Mayflower*, p. 332.

[24] Taylor, p. 201.

[25] Id.

[26] *Mendon, Massachusetts 1667-1967*, p. 35.

[27] Hurd, *History of Worcester County*, p. 377.

[28] Id., p. 36; *Rawson Family Memoir*, pp. 12-14. Rev. Grindal Rawson's daughter Mary married her father's successor in the Mendon pulpit, Rev. Joseph Dorr, who served for 52 years and whose son Joseph played a prominent role for Mendon in the American Revolution.

[29] *Annals of Mendon*, p. 185; Hurd, *History of Worcester County*, p. 377. Other parts of The Farm remained in Mendon. *The Town of Bellingham, Massachusetts 1719-1969*, at p. 7.

[30] Id.

[31] Borneman, *The French and Indian War*, pp. 6-13.

[32] Hurd, *History of Worcester County*, p. 379.

[33] *Historic & Archeological Resources of Central Massachusetts: A Framework for Preservation Decisions*. Massachusetts Historical Commission, February 1985, at p. 87; *Rawson Family Memoir*, p. 18.

[34] *Mendon, Massachusetts*, p. 49.

[35] Id., p. 51.

[36] Chernow, *Washington, A Life*, at pp. 516-19; Morison, *American People*, pp. 301-05; *George Washington: Writings*, p. 634. Washington and others were concerned about how the rioting (which was not limited to Massachusetts) would affect foreign governments' view of the American experiment. The crisis, along with other episodes, hastened the path toward a stronger federal government in the Constitutional Convention of 1787.

[37] *Massachusetts Historical Commission*, pp. 92, 101-02.

[38] Mathews, pp. 259-60.

[39] *Mendon, Massachusetts*, pp. 47, 59.

[40] Edward's brother William (the fourth consecutive William) died in the French and Indian War and another brother, Jonathan, moved to Pennsylvania. Other brothers Thomas, John and Perne all remained in Mendon or surrounding towns as Edward did. *Rawson Family Memoir*, pp. 29, 46-47.

[41] Rawsonville each year hosts the Rawson Family Association reunion, which in recent years passed its 100th year of gathering a number of Secretary Edward Rawson's descendants.

[42] For some, southwestern Vermont would be only a way station on their road to attractive farmlands in western New York.

III.
NORTH TO VERMONT:
MENDON TO PITTSFORD

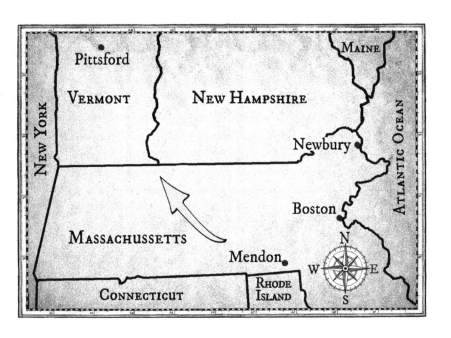

A s the sun rises high over Camel's Hump, the surface of Lake Champlain sparkles, a thousand diamonds of sun-light dancing on the gentle swells. From a vantage point on the shore of Northwest Bay in Westport, New York, a vista opens far northeast down the Narrows to distant Mount Mansfield, Vermont's tallest peak. Closer at hand, one looks southeast three miles across the lake to Button Bay and the Green Mountains that give Vermont its name. Gulls, great herons, osprey and the occasional bald eagle fly overhead, while an assortment of sailboats, powerboats, canoes and kayaks share the lake with ring-necked loons, diving cormorants and honking Canada geese.

The lakescape itself has not changed much in hundreds or even several thousands of years (if one ignores the cottages and houses peeking out from the tree-lined, rocky shores on both sides of Champlain). But the vessels cutting across this stretch of the lake certainly have changed. And, with a little imagination, it is possible to recreate some of the dramatic panoramas of the past as they would have been seen from this picturesque spot on Northwest Bay.

Birchbark war canoes came slipping silently past Split Rock and southward up the Narrows in 1609, carrying dozens of painted Algonquin warriors of the Montagnais tribe and their new champion, Frenchman Samuel de Champlain, on their way to confront their Iroquois enemies somewhere near Ticonderoga. With Champlain killing the chief of the bow-wielding Mohawk Iroquois with a blast from his arquebus, the Algonquins triumphed, one battle in an ongoing tribal conflict over boundaries and hunting lands. The Iroquois would eventually find their own powerful foreign champion in the English traders and colonists, and the contest for North America would be on.

The French dominated the lake for a time with their forts and battlements at Carillon (Ticonderoga), Saint-Frederic (Crown Point), Ile aux Noix and down the Richelieu River valley throughout the first half of the eighteenth century and the early stages of the French and Indian War. But Northwest Bay would see critical naval movements again in 1759 and 1760. British General Jeffrey Amherst drove the French north, forcing them to abandon and destroy Fort Carillon at Ticonderoga and Fort Saint-Frederic at Crown Point and to fall back past Northwest Bay all the way to the great islands at the north end of the lake.

In October 1759 Amherst sent Commodore Joshua Loring north with the war sloops *Boscawen* and *Duke of Cumberland* to trap the French and take control of the lake before retiring for the winter. The British thrust to take Montreal came in the campaigning season of 1760. An expeditionary force of more than 400 boats and 3400 men streamed north down the lake from Crown Point past our vantage point on Northwest Bay and through the Narrows, joining up with the larger British sloops in what has been described as "two four mile long columns on the lake," one of the largest combined military forces ever assembled on Lake Champlain. After taking Ile aux Noix just down the Richelieu River from the lake, the British forced the surrender of Montreal and became masters of Canada.

Less than twenty years later, under gray October skies in 1776, a half-dozen tattered and leaking boats led by Benedict Arnold's galley, *Congress*, could have been seen making their slow way south out of the Narrows, sailing and sweeping anxiously past Northwest Bay as several well-rigged British warships gave chase. The American and British sides had battled at Valcour Island near the New York shore the previous day. Outgunned and facing certain defeat, Arnold used the cover of night and fog to escape the British blockade, but now some of the royal navy ships were closing fast and firing volleys. Realizing he had no chance to beat the British to the safety of American shore batteries at Crown Point, Arnold made for the Vermont shore at Ferris Bay near Panton and scuttled his five remaining boats to keep them and their cannons out of British hands.

In 1814 the triumphant fleet sailing south up the Narrows and visible from Northwest Bay belonged to the Americans,

not the British. Captain Thomas Macdonough's brilliant victory over His Majesty's Lake Champlain command at the
Battle of Cumberland Bay at Plattsburgh, New York, blunted
another British thrust up the lake in another war. The shipbuild-
ers at Vergennes, Vermont would have swelled with pride as
Macdonough brought the fleet they'd built up the Narrows on
his way south to Whitehall, New York, accompanied by the prizes
taken from George III.

Stretching 120 miles from Whitehall in the south to the
mouth of the Richelieu River and Canada in the north, Lake
Champlain was more than just a waterway for warriors and their
navies. It provided a western coast of New England, bounding
the New England lands opened up for settlement especially
after the Revolution, and a magnet for immigrants from New
Hampshire, Connecticut, New York and Massachusetts. A number of Rawsons would be among those migrating from southern
Massachusetts to the new frontier of Vermont, one of them to the
small town of Pittsford nestled in the Otter Creek valley east of
the mountains.

✳   ✳   ✳   ✳

They were there first. The great migration of Asiatic
peoples into North and South America placed families,
tribes and nations of what would be called "Indians"
in every part of both continents, from the Aleutians to Tierra
del Fuego, including what would much later become New
England. Spear tips and arrowheads place these earliest settlers near Lake Champlain and the Green Mountains thousands of years before the first Europeans made landfall on the
Atlantic coast. Broadly speaking, to the north and east of the
lake, most of the natives were of various Algonquin tribes like
the Abenaki, the Montagnais or the Narraganset, while to the
south and west the Mohawks were the easternmost of the five
nations of the Iroquois.

Northern New England and eastern Canada make up the
land of the Western Abenaki, part of the Algonquin peoples,
and Lake Champlain was the "sacred center" of their universe.[1]
Before the Europeans came and upset the balance of their lives,
the Abenakis used the land for hunting as well as raising crops.
They were a mobile people, and their places followed the variations of the seasons: from a fertile green valley area for growing
food; to a stony lake front for fishing and hunting; to a secure
place for winter quarters as the weather turned cold; and returning to old village locations to plant new crops in the spring.
Lands that appeared abandoned by them in one season would
be revisited and reused in another. The Abenaki and their kin
would have had difficulty understanding why these rich, productive lands were thought by the European latecomers to be empty
and unclaimed, theirs for the taking.

The Europeans began to upend the native world of North
America in the sixteenth and seventeenth centuries, as described
earlier. Conquest was the Spanish way in the south, driven by the
hunger for gold, and they destroyed highly sophisticated native
empires in the Aztecs of Mexico and the Incas of Peru. But when
the French came up the great river they called the St. Lawrence
in the sixteenth century and created settlements at Quebec and
later Montreal, they were interested primarily in obtaining furs
for export to France. They explored west to the great lakes and
south on rivers large and small, and created a network of contacts
with natives to funnel the fur trade east and north to Montreal,
where French ships came to pick up furs and drop off supplies.
The competing Dutch fur trade began with Henry Hudson's
exploration up another great river in 1609 and the subsequent
creation of trading outposts centered on the Albany area and the
Mahican tribe (later violently displaced in their lands and their
trade by the fierce Mohawks). The English, too, traded for furs
with the Mahicans and others from their early settlements in
southern New England.

Trade, of course, by definition goes two ways. Shiny beads,
woven cloth and metal tools, fish hooks and utensils were valued

by the natives. But they valued more the firearms the Europeans could provide, both to make their hunting more successful and to give them an advantage in the frequent wars among the tribes. Although the English tried to discourage traders from providing weapons to the natives, such caution could not hold up when the Dutch or the French were more than willing to arm the Indians. Some European traders also found it helpful to provide brandy or rum to facilitate trade negotiations, creating another source of destabilization of the native ways. The fur trade proved a Faustian bargain for the natives. The ravenous European demand for furs led to greater (and now better armed) intertribal conflict as tribes, pressed by the newcomers, expanded into each other's traditional territories to seek more beaver, fox, mink and other valued fur-bearing animals.

Wars in Europe (and they were many and almost constant) became wars in North America as the French, English and Dutch (until displaced by the English in 1664) expected and encouraged their Indian trading partners to become allies in battle against their enemies, just as the Montagnais had enlisted Champlain against the Mohawks in 1609. Hot conflicts in Europe could be sure to spread flames in North America as well.

It was not European warfare, however, but European diseases that devastated the Western Abenaki in what would later become Vermont. While southern New England tribes were stricken by smallpox and other diseases by 1620, northern New England fell under the cruel scythe in 1633 and repeatedly thereafter. Historians estimate the mortality rate for the Western Abenaki and other tribes in northern New England was as high as 90 to 95 percent. Professor Colin G. Calloway summarized the situation well: "The introduction of Old World diseases among New World populations constituted an invasion more deadly than any carried out with fire and sword."[2] But there was also plenty of fire and sword.

The contested century from 1665 to 1763 determined the fate of the North American continent. As they explored and established trade through western waters, the French decided to fortify the vulnerable route to Lake Champlain in the south. A French fort built on Isle La Motte in 1666 at the northern end of the lake has been described as "the first European colonial settlement within the boundaries" of what would later become Vermont.[3] After the devastation of King Philip's War in 1675-76, many Indians abandoned or were driven from southern New England, and the relentless English settlers created new borders reaching ever farther north. French and Indian raids into the newly settled areas, like the devastating attack on Deerfield, Massachusetts in 1704, led to calls for greater protection of the frontier settlements, and those demands increased during the four years of what was called "Grey Lock's War" from 1724 to 1727.

Abetted by the French, the Abenaki chief Grey Lock con-ducted a series of raids down the Connecticut River, seeking to roll back the English expansion especially around Northfield, Massachusetts. Dozens of settlers were killed or taken captive by the raiders, who would quickly disappear back to the north. Fort Dummer, constructed in 1724 at their far northern settle-ments by the Massachusetts Bay Colony, became "the first per-manent English settlement in Vermont."[4] Situated at present day Brattleboro and named for the colony's lieutenant governor, Fort Dummer provided settlers with some degree of protection during Grey Lock's War, as well as a stronghold from which colonists could mount brutal retaliatory raids of their own.[5] In later, less dangerous times the fort would also serve as a trading post. Grey Lock was never defeated by the English, but an uneasy peace was restored after 1727 and continued until around 1744.[6]

Troubled by the rapid northward and westward expansion of English settlements, the French command in Montreal decided to plant the flag of New France further south on Lake Champlain. Choosing the narrow strait at Crown Point from which all pas-sage up or down the lake could be controlled, the French built a wooden stockade on the eastern shore in 1731 and later began work on a substantial stone fortress on the western side. Fort Saint-Frederic, with its impressive four story stone tower inside battlements protected by four bastions, soon became the center of a small French settlement and a source of great concern to the English in Massachusetts.

An arms race of fort building ensued. By 1754 there were French or British forts strategically positioned throughout North America. The French forts protected the St. Lawrence (Louisbourg, Quebec, Montreal), Lake Champlain (Saint-Frederic), the Great Lakes (Frontenac, Niagara, Presque Isle, Detroit, Michilimackinac) and the Ohio and Mississippi Rivers (Duquesne, Chartres, New Orleans). The British positioned forces on the Hudson (Edward), Lake George (William Henry), Lake Ontario (Oswego) and the Appalachian frontier (Cumberland, Prince George).

War was inevitable as the eighteenth century reached its midpoint, in North America as well as in Europe and beyond, and it was none other than George Washington who lit the fuse.[7] A twenty-one year old Virginia militia captain who had explored and surveyed on the frontier, Washington was charged in late 1753 with delivering to the French fort in the Ohio valley an ultimatum demanding their evacuation of these "British" lands. After carrying back to Williamsburg the letter of refusal of the French, Washington was tasked in 1754 with fortifying the area against French incursions. The French and their Indian allies defeated Washington's meager troops and he was forced to surrender Fort Necessity before being permitted to return to Williamsburg.

The conflict rapidly expanded. Back in London, William Pitt and the king's military advisors devised a North American war strategy based on separate thrusts up the St. Lawrence, north on Lake Champlain, on Lakes Ontario and Erie, and west through Virginia to the Appalachians. When the cocksure General Edward Braddock landed at Alexandria, Virginia with several hundred redcoat regulars in 1755, he intended to put the French quickly in their place and show the colonials how to fight. But he fared no better than Washington in a battle near the Monongahela River and Fort Duquesne, and died in the effort. Washington, who accompanied the British as an colonial adjutant to Braddock, successfully rallied the survivors and led them to safety, restoring his military reputation at least among the Virginians.

The war continued to go poorly for the British in North America over the next two years, even as new fronts opened up overseas after the rival nations formally declared war. The British lost battles on the Mediterranean and in Germany in 1757, and were forced to surrender Fort Oswego on Lake Ontario and Fort William Henry on Lake George. The latter site turned into a bloody massacre of British wounded and captured prisoners by the Abenaki and other allies of the French, whom the French failed to control, with more than 700 casualties. (This episode provided the basis for James Fenimore Cooper's fictional *Last of the Mohicans*.)

One more military disaster awaited the British before the tide would turn in 1758. Poor leadership and worse tactics led the British to march in formation up a well-defended hill outside Fort Carillon (Ticonderoga) on the New York side of Lake Champlain, where they were cut to pieces by the grossly outnumbered French defenders and forced to withdraw. Nearly two thousand redcoats were killed or wounded.

Promoted from colonel to major general in 1758 and given charge of Britain's war in North America, Jeffrey Amherst arrived just in time to oversee the capture of the French fortress at Louisbourg in Nova Scotia (with troops led by Brigadier General James Wolfe). By the end of the year, the British had also taken Fort Frontenac near the Thousand Islands at the mouth of Lake Ontario and Fort Duquesne on the Ohio River. The British momentum in North America continued in 1759 with the surrender of Fort Niagara, and Amherst's overwhelming command then forced the French to abandon Fort Carillon and Fort Saint-Frederic before retreating north on Lake Champlain, blowing up both forts to deny the British their munitions and use. Amherst immediately began construction of an English fortress at Crown Point, the location of which at a choke point of Lake Champlain he described as "the finest situation, I think, that I have seen in America."[8] The way to Canada was now open.

The British also found success in the other fronts of what has been called "the first truly world war."[9] In Senegal, in India, in the West Indies, in the Bay of Biscay and in the Philippines, the British Empire took shape as losses mounted for the French and their European allies over the next few years. Back in North America, General Amherst recognized that he needed a better way to get men and materiel to Lake Champlain if he was to be successful in expelling the French. In 1759, as Amherst planned his invasion route north, he sent Captain John Stark and 200 Rangers to survey and cut a road from the east side of Lake Champlain at Chimney Point (named for the visible remains of the old French settlement) to the southeast along the valleys of Otter Creek and the Black River to Fort Number Four on the Connecticut River. The route followed an old Indian path through the valleys, swamps and mountain passes.

By 1760 the "Crown Point Road" stretched more than 77 miles, with a width of about 20 feet, using logs to create a corduroy roadbed through the swampy areas. (An important strategic improvement for the British in the French and Indian War, the road played even a greater role for the rebellious colonists against the British during the American Revolution. But the real significance of the Crown Point Road would come between the wars, after the French were repulsed and their Indian allies pushed back toward Canada. After the peace treaty of 1763, settlers from Massachusetts and Connecticut used the road to penetrate deep into the newly opened frontier. A new means of migration had opened up new lands to settlement.)

The fall of Canada was inevitable if not immediate. The French surrender of Quebec in 1759 after the deaths of both sides' commanders, Generals Wolfe and Montcalm, in battle on the Plains of Abraham left Montreal vulnerable. Amherst's combined naval and land forces, as described earlier, swept northward in 1760 to make the British the masters of all of North America, at least as far as the French were concerned.

France's Indian allies were not so ready to concede. After the Treaty of Paris formally turned Canada over to the British in

1763 without addressing the rights of native North Americans, the King issued a Proclamation that was intended to set the rules governing the vast lands newly taken from the French. Royal governors were prohibited from making land grants beyond the Appalachians, despite the fact that colonial settlement and speculation in those lands had already begun. It would soon become clear that no piece of paper signed in London could change the rapidly advancing reality on the ground.[10]

But that will become part of this story when it moves to Michigan. As to Vermont, the end of the French and Indian War opened a new era in land grants and rapid movement of settlers from populated southern and eastern New England. As described by historian Calloway, "victory over the French broke the dike, initiating the fifteen year period of migration, land speculation, and settlement in northern New England [described as] 'the great swarming time.'"[11] Many of those settlers and speculators rushed northward into the lands known only, at that time, as the "New Hampshire Grants."

When the province of New Hampshire was created by royal proclamation in 1741, separating it from Massachusetts, an important detail was left unaddressed -- the location of its western border. Massachusetts had claimed all of the lands west to within 20 miles of the Hudson River, the same boundary as existed between New York and Connecticut. New York, in turn, claimed all of the lands east to the Connecticut River, based on the 1664 royal grant to the Duke of York. Millions of acres sat in the area of the overlapping provincial claims. The first royal governor of New Hampshire, Benning Wentworth, had every incentive to assume the correctness of the Massachusetts claim, to which his new colony succeeded. Land held value, especially for a greedy governor whose province needed money and who could use the land to build his wealth at the same time.

Beginning with Bennington (which he proudly named for himself), Governor Wentworth initiated a series of land grants in 1749 after notifying New York of his plans. Each new township held thirty-six square miles, subdivided into lots awarded to well-placed grantees who typically sold the lots for a profit rather than settling on them. Wentworth would typically reserve lots for himself in the grants, eventually accumulating 65,000 acres in his own name. Between 1749 and 1764, Governor Wentworth granted charters for 129 townships north of the Massachusetts border, the first 16 on the western side of the Connecticut River but the later ones reaching all the way to the lands New Hampshire claimed to be the western border with New York. These "New Hampshire Grants," as they came to be known, covered three million acres of valley, forest and mountain lands.[12]

After New York objected to the grants as illegal and therefore of no effect, the competing royal provinces of New Hampshire and New York submitted their boundary dispute to the King. But the wheels of the royal bureaucracy turned slowly and years passed without a decision. Wentworth waited a while before eventually resumed his grant making. Finally, in 1764 a royal order was issued affirming the New York position that the Connecticut River bounded New Hampshire and that the grants were invalid. New York's Governor Cadwallader Colden immediately began to grant overlapping land patents in the territory; settlers who had moved in and made improvements in the land on the basis of the New Hampshire grants were invited to pay for their land a second time, this time to New York, or face eviction. Confronted with the very real prospect of losing their lands and their homes, the New Hampshire grantees organized their opposition and sent representatives to London to plead the equities of their case.

These efforts resulted in a second order from London in 1767, this one directing the New York authorities to hold off on making further grants or dispossessing the New Hampshire grantees until the matter could be considered again by the King. New York's then Governor Henry Moore held off as directed for two years, but his successor Governor Colden (again) changed New York's position in 1769 by issuing new grants to New Yorkers and encouraging action to dispossess the New Hampshire grantees.

When New York patent holders brought suit in New York in 1770 to press their claims, the New Hampshire settlers thought they would have a fair opportunity to assert their prior grants and seek an equitable resolution, but the court refused to permit the New Hampshire grants into evidence and ruled for the New Yorkers. Having failed to gain protection either from the King or from the provincial courts, the New Hampshire Grants settlers took matters into their own hands. At a meeting at the Catamount Tavern in Bennington in 1771, a group of the settlers agreed to protect their lands from the Yorkers, by force if necessary. If one event can be pointed to as the beginning of the separate state of Vermont, this was it. When the New York sheriff tried to enforce the court's orders, he was firmly turned away by well-armed settlers. When New York surveyors set up to define property lines for the New York patent holders, they were confronted and expelled, sometimes with the threat of violence and sometimes with whippings, tar and feathers, and death threats.

First in Bennington and then spreading throughout the western Grants, settlers formed "committees of safety" and began to coordinate their opposition to the New York authorities. Ethan Allen and what soon became known as the Green Mountain Boys led the effort to protect the settlers against New York through armed opposition where necessary. As the disputes and occasional violence continued to escalate, New York passed punitive measures in 1774 declaring the opposition outlaws and authorizing penalties, including execution, without trial for those who hindered New York officials in pressing New York claims.[13] Settlers in the Grants responded by gathering in a convention which declared itself responsible for the government of the Grants, separate from either New York or New Hampshire authorities, until the King resolved the boundary and property disputes.

A violent confrontation was inevitable, and it came in March of 1775 at the Westminster courthouse. A New York judge attempted to conduct court and to hear cases that included claims against New Hampshire debtors. Settlers from the Grants took over the courthouse temporarily but were attacked and expelled by New York authorities after a brief battle in which two of the settlers were fatally wounded. The countryside quickly rose up and the Green Mountain Boys retook the courthouse, arrested the judge and other New Yorkers and packed them off to a Massachusetts jail. The "Westminster Massacre" galvanized opposition to New York throughout the Grants, but a final resolution of the dispute would have to wait. The Minutemen of Lexington and Concord saw to that.[14]

The British posed a much greater threat to the settlers in the New Hampshire Grants than did the New Yorkers. Within weeks of the "Shot Heard Round the World," plans were made to capture the British-held forts at Ticonderoga and Crown Point along with the cannons defending them. While Benedict Arnold raised money and troops in Massachusetts to attack the forts, Ethan Allen and the Green Mountain Boys decided to move quickly against the lightly defended British positions. Arnold caught up with Allen as the assault was being finalized and, after asserting and failing to gain acknowledgment of his superior claim to leadership, joined Allen's successful early morning raid. The capture of Crown Point quickly followed.[15] Arnold and a small group took one of the captured British schooners north down the lake to St. John, surprising the British with their daring raid and making off with another schooner. Allen made a more aggressive and foolhardy attempt to take the fort at St. John, despite Arnold's warning that it was well-defended, but he was met by British reinforcements and had to make a disorganized retreat.

The Americans kept a tenuous hold on the lake into the fall of 1776, when they learned that Sir Guy Carleton was preparing a major assault with both land and naval forces. General Horatio Gates instructed Arnold (who had been a merchant captain in private life before the war) to build and deploy ships to block Carleton. With his hastily assembled fleet of fifteen vessels (including the three taken from the British at Ticonderoga and St. John in 1775), Arnold sailed north from Whitehall, eventually choosing a defensive position behind Valcour Island ten miles south of Plattsburgh to await the enemy. Substantially outgunned by the larger British fleet, Arnold's crews managed to use their wind-protected position to survive the day long onslaught (though losing two of their ships in the battle), and then escaped the blockade that night by rowing past the British lines under the cover of fog and darkness. Chased hard and recognizing that he could not manage to get to the protective guns of Crown Point (as four of his ships were able to do), Arnold scuttled his remaining boats on the Vermont side and brought most of his men safely behind American lines.

Fortunately for the Revolution, after probing further south toward now well-defended Ticonderoga and fighting driving winds, Carleton decided against pressing his advantage. He chose to defer the planned invasion until the next campaign season in the spring of 1777. The delay would prove fatal to Britain's northern strategy.

Under General John Burgoyne, more than seven thousand British troops advanced south largely unopposed in June 1777. They retook Ticonderoga without a battle after the Americans made the strategic error of failing to fortify the nearby heights of Mount Defiance, leaving Ticonderoga indefensible. While Burgoyne waited for anticipated support from Lord Howe in the south, which never came, he sent a large contingent to pursue the Americans near Hubbardton on the eastern side of Champlain. Despite a valiant stand by the Green Mountain Boys, now commanded by Seth Warner, the Americans were forced to give up the field after considerable losses and fell back to reorganize.

With an urgent need for supplies and no sign of Howe's promised second front, Burgoyne learned that the Americans had stores of supplies and farm stock to the south in Bennington, Vermont. Several hundred German mercenaries under Lieutenant Colonel Frederick Baum made their way toward Bennington in August, but this time the Americans under General John Stark were ready for them. A fierce battle on a hill overlooking the Waloomsac River and the timely arrival of reinforcements under Seth Warner enabled the Americans to inflict more than 200 casualties and take 700 prisoners. This disastrous result left

Burgoyne's British troops no choice but to continue south on the New York side, still undersupplied and without reinforcements. After taking further losses in the two furious battles at Freeman's Farm (in which Benedict Arnold heroically led American attacks and suffered grievous wounds), with his supply line cut off and no prospect of reinforcements, Burgoyne was forced to surrender his army at Saratoga on October 16, giving the Americans the most significant victory of the war to that point.[16]

While the central stage of the Revolution moved south after Saratoga, American settlers in the Grants were not free of incursions from the Canada-based British and their native allies. Middlebury, Brandon and Royalton all suffered calamitous raids, and the Vermont Committee of Safety warned settlers north of Pittsford and Rutland they could not be protected. Many to the north had to abandon their farms and move south to seek protection behind American lines.

The experience of defending their homes and farms against the British, organizing their own governance through the committees of safety during the War, and acting as a full partner in American military affairs in the region hardened the attitudes of many Grants' settlers against New York or anyone else who threatened their rights and their land titles. In what has been characterized by some historians as "the revolution within the Revolution," the Grants declared their own independence, flirted with rejoining Great Britain and, eventually, became the fourteenth state of the American union in 1791.

The years between 1777 and 1791 would provide for entire volumes of fascinating Vermont history, far beyond the scope of this narrative. At Windsor in 1777, delegates declared that the New Hampshire Grants were a separate district, independent of New York and New Hampshire. They petitioned the Continental Congress to recognize their independent status and treat them as a new state, but New York's objection succeeded in preventing such a result. Undaunted, and having adopted the name of Vermont, a convention of delegates met in Windsor in June 1777, approved a declaration of rights and began to write a constitution to govern themselves. It became effective in March 1778. Also in 1778, Vermont annexed sixteen townships in New Hampshire but then reversed itself when it became clear that the expansion would prejudice Vermont before the Continental Congress. Vermonters were encouraged when the Congress announced in 1779 that it would conduct hearings on the competing claims of Vermont, New York, New Hampshire and Massachusetts, but disappointed when the hearings resulted in no decision.

As Congress dithered, the British seized the initiative, applying violence and diplomacy to try to turn the Vermonters against the American cause. British troops in 1780 reoccupied Crown Point and Ticonderoga on Lake Champlain and attacked as far south as Fort Ann, Fort Edward and Fort George in New York. A brutal raid on Royalton, Vermont followed in October.

But the British then used the threat of further incursions to open discussions with Vermont's leaders about having the territory abandon the Revolution and recommit itself to Britain in return for peace and the guarantee of its land titles. The so-called "Haldimand Negotiations" (named for Frederick Haldimand, the British governor general of Canada who led them) engaged Ethan and Ira Allen as well as Vermont's Governor Thomas Chittendon and other leaders in serious discussions about Vermont's future. Janus-like, the Vermonters looked both north and south at the same time. Were these men truly considering the British proposal or were they simply trying to buy time and put pressure on the Continental Congress to admit Vermont as a separate state? Historians disagree. But General Washington was among those who feared the worst and recognized the critical importance of retaining Vermont's loyalty. Vermont again complicated the debate in Congress by deciding to annex not only thirty-five New Hampshire towns but also fourteen in New York, creating a "Greater Vermont" and continuing discussions with the British.

In 1781, Congress finally moved toward recognizing Vermont's claims of independence from New York, New Hampshire and Massachusetts, but only if Greater Vermont were undone. The Vermont legislature at first refused in 1781,

but when the issue was taken up again in 1782 (and confront-
ing the real prospect of armed conflict with New Hampshire and
New York), General Washington turned the tide with a letter
to Governor Chittendon strongly encouraging Vermont to abandon its annexations or face military intervention. The lawmak-
ers seized upon Washington's assertion that this would open the
door to treatment as a separate state and took action in February
1782 to dissolve the unions with the New Hampshire townships
in the east and the New York townships in the west. But when
the Continental Congress formally voted whether to approve
Vermont's application for statehood, in April 1782, six states
objected and Vermont continued to be an unhappy orphan.

Vermont remained outside the new United States for nine
more years. Finally, under the leadership of Governor Moses
Robinson and with the considerable assistance of Alexander
Hamilton, negotiations with New York to resolve issues of
compensation for land titles were successful in removing that
important obstacle. Regional politics provided the final impe-
tus for statehood, as northern states feared that the admission
of Kentucky (to be birthed from Virginia) without a northern
counterpart would shift the balance of power in Congress. After
Vermont acted in 1791 to ratify the Constitution of the United
States, Congress approved the admission of Vermont as the fourteenth state (and Kentucky as the fifteenth).

The fertile soils of Vermont's valleys had long been a magnet drawing a few hardy settlers north from the established colonies. But the ever-present dangers to life and property had been
too great for most. After the construction of Fort Dummer in
1724 and the end of Grey Lock's War three years later, a trickle
of immigrants had begun. Fierce conflict with the French and
their Abenaki allies in the 1740s discouraged all but a few. As an
unsteady peace began and Governor Wentworth started making
his township grants in 1749, more immigrants began to arrive,
but it was not until the end of the French and Indian War in
1763 that large numbers of settlers made their way north and
began to clear the forest for farmlands. In the evocative words

of Vermont historians Michael Sherman, Gene Sessions and P. Jeffrey Potash: "When the Treaty of Paris in 1763 confirmed the French loss of Canada, the Vermont forests already echoed to the clank of the surveyor's chain and the ring of the settlers' axes."[17]

Their numbers increased quickly, from 1000 in 1764, to 4000 in 1768, to 7000 in 1771 and to more than 12,000 by 1774. With the end of the American Revolution and the elimination of the British threat, the floodgates opened. There were 30,000 people in Vermont by 1780, nearly 85,000 by 1790 and an astonishing 217,895 identified in the 1810 census.[18]

Where did these immigrants come from and what drew them north? Cheap land in a nation of farmers is the simplest answer. In 1790, according to the census, 95% of all Americans lived on farms.[19] Land had always been inexpensive in the Grants because of the uncertainty of land titles, as New York asserted its claims with threats and political maneuvers.[20] Even after that issue was resolved and Vermont admitted to the Union, however, land values remained better in Vermont than in neighboring states and the land showed great fertility for cash crops like wheat. Massachusetts, Connecticut and New York contributed the greatest number of immigrants into Vermont, but many also came from New Jersey, New Hampshire and other states. Just as the newcomers from England had often named their new towns after the homes they left behind, the names of towns in Vermont can often be connected to the location from which large numbers of settlers had come: Rutland, Barre and Mendon, to name just a few.

If cheap land was the factor pulling immigrants into Vermont, indebtedness and taxes in their home states also provided a push for many settlers. Economic times were hard in the new United States after gaining independence, as foreign trade had to be rebuilt and manufacturing industries suffered from cheap British imports. The burden of heavy debt and high taxes caused some to take up arms to prevent creditors and bankruptcy courts from seizing their lands. Shays's Rebellion in Massachusetts was the most visible but not the only example of this, and it was to

Vermont that Shays and others escaped after their short-lived insurrection was put down.

Pittsford, Vermont was one of the townships whose population swelled in the years following the Revolution. Governor Wentworth had made the grant for Pittsford in 1761, on land situated just north of Rutland in central Vermont. One of the largest rivers in western Vermont, Otter Creek, runs through the town and its mile wide valley provided fertile farmland. Other land in town, set on hillsides and mountains, was found to be more suitable for the grazing of sheep. The name Pittsford reflected the settlement's position at the best ford on Otter Creek, and honored the "Great Commoner," William Pitt, who oversaw Great Britain's victory over France and Spain in the Seven Years War and who later became an advocate for the American colonials. A popular hunting area of the natives, Pittsford was explored by the English who fought the French and their native allies in the 1730s and 1740s, and was later traversed by General Amherst's military road from Fort Number Four on the Connecticut River to Crown Point on Lake Champlain.

First settlers Gideon and Benjamin Cooley came to Pittsford in 1767 from Greenwich, Massachusetts and settled their families in 1769. Seven more families arrived in 1770.[21] Among the many who followed, Eleazer Harwood moved to Pittsford in 1776 from Bennington, where he had been one of the earliest settlers to join Solomon Robinson[22] and others from Hardwick, Massachusetts ten years before. Other newcomers arrived in Pittsford from Massachusetts, Connecticut and New York as well as from different towns in the Grants territory.[23]

Pittsford found itself uncomfortably close to the British invasion route in 1777. Many residents were forced to flee as the British came through neighboring Hubbardton. Upon returning, they decided a fort was essential to their security and constructed the stockade they called Fort Mott near Otter Creek. As Indian raids continued to strike Pittsford, a larger fort was built about a mile from the first; Fort Vengeance could garrison more than 150 troops to defend the area.

The town continued to grow with the end of the Revolution. By the time Vermont became the fourteenth state in 1791, there were 850 residents in Pittsford. This increased to over 1400 souls by 1800 and more than 1900 by 1810, but then the population remained essentially flat for the next 70 years. The early settlers constructed grist mills and saw mills, and commerce grew with a fulling mill, a cloth factory and a marble quarry all in operation by 1800.

One of the many newcomers was Leonard Rawson, a fifth generation descendant of Secretary Rawson, who moved to Pittsford from Mendon, Massachusetts in 1800. Several of his first cousins from Mendon had made the move to southern Vermont and this may have influenced Leonard's decision to resettle.[24] He purchased 96 acres of the "Harwood Farm" from Israel Keith, and married Lydia Hitchcock, a daughter of John Hitchcock who had brought his family to Vermont from Saybrook, Connecticut in 1785. Rawson farmed and also worked as a joiner or carpenter building wooden structures in town. The house he built for himself, now gone, stood not far from the location of the schoolhouse for Pittsford District No. 2 on the south side of town.[25]

The turbulent years between 1810 and 1830 changed Vermont as well as the rest of the young American republic. War and its aftermath, disease, environmental catastrophe, technological innovation and Adam Smith's invisible hand, all contributed to turn the tide of migration in Vermont from flow to ebb. For decades settlers had rushed into Vermont; now they began to leave in even greater numbers.

A rocky post-revolutionary relationship with Great Britain turned ugly in the first decade of the nineteenth century, as President Jefferson and the Congress deemed it necessary to confront British high seas aggression with an economic embargo that hurt American business more than it damaged Britain's. Many Vermont traders turned to smuggling (some using a route still called "Smuggler's Notch" near Mount Mansfield) to maintain their lucrative dealings with British Canada, and their illicit business continued even after war was declared between the United

States and Great Britain in 1812. As in the prior century, however, Vermont soon found that its proximity to Canada and the water highway of Lake Champlain, so advantageous for trade in times of peace, became a dangerous liability in times of war.

What historians have described as "the strongest, best disciplined, and most completely equipped army the British ever sent to North America" came south from Montreal in 1814.[26] Accompanied by a naval flotilla of seventeen ships, the invaders stopped at Plattsburgh, New York, confronted by a much smaller American land force but a nearly equal lake fleet newly built at Vergennes and commanded by Captain Thomas Macdonough. The young captain's strategic and tactical decision-making combined with the seamanship and bravery of his inexperienced sailors to devastate the British squadron at the battle of Plattsburgh Bay on September 11, 1814. Forced to strike their colors after taking heavy losses, the British surrendered. Governor-general Prevost, suddenly lacking both naval protection and an assured supply route on Lake Champlain, decided to turn his huge army back to Montreal. The Americans had won a hugely important victory, one of the very few successful campaigns in this war.[27] Peace was successfully negotiated a few months later.

But removal of the military threat did not mean peaceful trade relations. As British manufactured goods rushed back into the United States after the war, the nascent American manufacturing industry suffered greatly. In Vermont as elsewhere, sales fell, factories were shuttered and men were thrown out of work. Some chose to leave the state for better prospects.

Disease struck hard at the families of those who stayed. In 1804, in 1812 and again in 1813 epidemics swept the land. The 1813 spread of "lung fever" from Burlington to many other parts of the state is said to have killed more than 6000 Vermonters. Without modern antibiotics there was little to be done to break the wildfire of diseases like spotted fever or pneumonia. Children and the elderly were, as always, the most vulnerable, but even otherwise strong adults were not immune. Death notices became a common feature in the newspapers of the day.

Then the weather turned fiercely against New England.

On the other side of the Pacific Ocean, a volcano blew with a force not seen or heard in the last 10,000 years. Pyroclastic flows of gas and lava raced down the mountainside, clearing fields and villages, killing perhaps 10,000 people before they could escape. The smoke and steam from the blast pierced the clouds, rising more than 25 miles into the atmosphere. An estimated twelve cubic tons of ash and rocks, of gases and dust -- the top third of what had been a 13,000 foot high mountain -- flew into the sky, darkening the day and illuminating the night. Ten times as powerful as the eruption of Krakatoa in 1883, nearly twenty times as powerful as the blast at Mount St. Helens in 1980, the 1815 explosion of Mount Tambora on the South Sea island of Sumbawa changed lives as far away as the young United States as well as old Europe.

How did a volcano on the opposite side of the world, two-thirds of the way east on the Indonesian archipelago, devastate the livelihood of New Englanders more than eight thousand miles away and bring a deadly famine to northern Europe? Why was the period 1815-1816 called by Vermonters "Eighteen Hundred and Froze to Death" as well as "The Year Without a Summer"?

The most devastating impact of the enormous eruption obviously struck the islanders living near the peak and on the surrounding islands in what has been described as "by far the deadliest eruption in recorded history."[28] With dust and ash falling on their fields and killing their crops, an estimated 90,000 people died of starvation and disease within the first year in the region. But the particulates and aerosols thrown high into the stratosphere slowly circled the globe, remaining aloft and diminishing the sun for many months after the blast.

The climate was colder in 1815 than it is today. What scientists call the Little Ice Age extended from the fourteenth century into the nineteenth, with a peak around 1700, causing the mountain glaciers that are still seen in the Rockies or the Alps to have been much larger and more extensive. Some combination of Earth's orbital eccentricity, the tilt of its axis away from the sun in the northern hemisphere's winter, and periodic solar variations may be responsible for the cycle of "little ice ages" as well as for the longer cycle of "great ice ages" impacting the Earth. In any case, winters were longer and colder in the colonial era and for decades after independence.[29]

But the weather under the lingering haze of the Tambora eruption went from unusual to bizarre. A mild winter turned into an erratic series of cold snaps and warm spells. Killing frosts struck hard at New England farmers' fields in May, June and in some areas even into July and August of 1816. Snow fell amidst a wave of cold in Vermont in June, and freezing weather and snow struck again in late August. Winter came back in September with more hard frosts and snow, leaving 1816 as the year without a summer. A newspaper in Windsor, Vermont observed in October: "It is extremely cold for the time of year. The late frosts have entirely killed the corn. It is not probable that enough will get ripe for seed next year. There is not sufficient hay to winter cattle upon and nothing with which to fatten them this fall."[30]

How cold was it? One analysis of temperature records found that: "Temperatures in New England generally ranged between two to seven degrees Fahrenheit below normal from May through September. More to the point, the sharpest declines from the norm occurred during the critical growing months of June and July."[31] The turn of the year brought no relief. Record cold weather struck New England again in January, and snowdrifts refused to give way to spring even into May in Vermont. Farmers in northern Europe experienced similar problems. Unusual snowfalls filled with Tambora's dust left red, yellow or brown snowdrifts in Italy and Hungary.[32] Torrential rains followed throughout Europe. Massive crop failures, especially in Ireland as near daily rains drowned the fields, created famine conditions that killed tens of thousands.

Farming was hard enough in the hilly country of Vermont without having to contend with the effects of volcanic eruptions in the South Pacific. Once, thousands of new settlers had come north from Massachusetts and Connecticut to lands opened up to migration by the end of the Revolutionary War. In the years after Tambora, many settlers left Vermont and New England to find new opportunity in the territory west of the Appalachians made accessible by the end of the War of 1812.

Technology and economics soon combined to deal Vermonters further setbacks. The canal craze of the 1820s opened not only the Erie Canal through upstate New York to Lake Erie but also the Champlain Canal connecting Lake Champlain with the Hudson River. Vermonters rejoiced as cheaper transportation for their goods opened new markets to the south, and towns like Burlington on the shores of Lake Champlain prospered as transportation centers. But those same new markets now opened for wheat farmers in western New York and in the Old Northwest, whose abundant harvests brought greater competition and lower prices. Vermont farmers reeled. The 1820s also saw Vermont pay a price for its over-reliance on wheat. The thin, rocky soils of much of Vermont were easily depleted in the best of times. Wheat had become the cash crop for many Vermont farmers, but harvest after harvest took a toll on the productivity of the fields dedicated to the grain. Wheat also proved vulnerable to disease and to insect infestation in the 1820s.

Vermont farmers who could afford to turned it a new cash crop: wool. The price of wool (which was driven up artificially and temporarily by the imposition of new federal tariffs in the 1820s) led many farmers to swap out their wheat fields for grazing lands, and the number of sheep and cattle in Vermont surged in what some call a "sheep mania."[33]

Higher land prices changed the face of farming, as small farms were sold and the number of farm jobs fell. People left the farms, and they left Vermont. Vermont's population had grown sharply between 1791 and 1810. But previously booming areas like Rutland county saw their growth level off over the next several decades, as people left in almost the same numbers as those who came in.[34]   In *Freedom and Unity*, the authors succinctly capture what was happening: "The rising market economy and increasing land prices, combined with a static number of

farms, permanently altered the broad pattern that had existed at
the turn of the century of independent yeomen farmers providing for themselves most of the necessities of life. Concurrently,
the prospects for agricultural hired hands also receded. Lacking
the opportunity, or the capital, to purchase a farm of their own,
these men in large numbers abandoned hopes for land ownership,
drifted to employment as small tradesmen, mechanics or factory workers in larger Vermont communities and southern New
England industrial towns, or abandoned the Green Mountains
for the West." [35]

In short, the seventy years between the 1760s and the 1830s
told the tale of migration into and out of Vermont. With the end
of the French and Indian War in 1763, English settlers rushed to
settle in the hills and valleys previously occupied by the Abenakis.
Although the Revolution spilled into Vermont with fierce raids
by the British and their Indian allies, the Peace of Paris and the
resolution of the New Hampshire Grants conflict with New York
opened the door wide to settlers seeking productive new farmland, reaching a peak by around 1810. But the outflow began
soon after, as Vermont suffered an economic downturn after the
War of 1812; another deadly epidemic in 1813; extreme weather
after 1816; a financial crisis in 1818; soil depletion and wheat
crop infestation; the disruptive transition to sheep farming; and
competition from wheat farmers in the Northwest after the Erie
Canal opened in 1825. In the face of all these challenges, and
with cheap land available beyond the lakes, many Vermonters fled
to the newly opened lands of the Old Northwest to begin anew.

✳ ✳ ✳ ✳

Early Pittsford resident Leonard Rawson's wife Lydia was
one of those who died during or soon after Vermont's
devastatingly hard year of 1816, and a daughter died as
well. Leonard outlived Lydia by only four years, leaving a young
family of two sons and four daughters orphaned in Vermont. All
but one of them would remain Vermonters, probably raised by

Lydia's sister Abigail and her husband David Hall [36] who also lived in Pittsford. One of the youngsters, though, yet another Edward Rawson, would eventually join the flood of migration to the west and a new home, in Michigan. One chapter in the Rawson story ended, and a new one began.

---

[1] Calloway, p. 12.

[2] Calloway, pp. 35, 36-37; Sherman, Sessions and Potash, *Freedom and Unity*, p. 40.

[3] Sherman et al, p.46

[4] Calloway, p. 26.

[5] Sherman et al, p. 55.

[6] Calloway, pp. 116-130.

[7] Horace Walpole later said that "the volley of a young Virginian in the backwoods of America set the world on fire." Quoted in Fischer and Kelly, p. 166. Some historians, however, point to the brutal French and Indian attack on the English settlement at Pickawillany on the Ohio frontier in 1752 as an earlier flash point which led to war. *See*, e.g., R. Douglas Hurt, *The Ohio Frontier*, pp. 33-35.

[8] Borneman, p. 202. Ironically, Amherst's British fort at Crown Point would serve for only twenty years before a fire and subsequent abandonment left a set of impressive ruins that can be visited to this day.

[9] Borneman, p. xi.

[10] George Washington wrote, cynically, that the settlement ban in the Royal Proclamation was "a temporary expedient to quiet the minds of the Indians." Quoted by Ronald Wright in *Stolen Continents*, p. 223.

[11] Calloway, p. 183.

[12] Sherman et al, pp. 73-75.

[13] Mello, *Moses Robinson and the Founding of Vermont*, p. 57.

[14] Mello, pp. 61-63.

[15] The cannons of Ticonderoga and Crown Point would play a critical role in driving the British out of Boston several months later. Colonel Henry Knox led an astonishing and successful effort to haul 120 cannons from Lake Champlain to the heights of Dorchester above Boston harbor. When the British recognized the peril to their fleet,

they negotiated a hasty retreat, leaving the grateful city in the hands of General Washington's troops.

[16] Despite suffering a serious injury to his leg during the battle, Benedict Arnold was the hero of Saratoga, leading his men in cutting off and defeating Burgoyne's attempted escape at the second battle of Freeman's Farm. General Gates minimized Arnold's contribution, leaving Arnold resentful and beginning his downward spiral into treason at West Point. *See* Philbrick, *George Washington, Benedict Arnold, and the Fate of the American Revolution*, pp. 167, 173.

[17] Sherman et al, p. 75.

[18] Sherman et al, pp. 81, 92, 625.

[19] Daniel, pp. 10-11.

[20] Sherman et al (at p. 78) state that the uncertainty of land titles caused land in the Grants to be less than one hundredth the price of comparable Maine lands and one four hundredth the price in rural Massachusetts. No wonder settlers flooded into the area.

[21] Smith and Rann, p. 730.

[22] When settlers in the Grants needed someone to plead the equity of their land claims against the New York colonial authorities, they asked Solomon Robinson to go to London to represent their interests. Robinson succeeded in obtaining an order from the Privy Council enjoining New York's enforcement of its claims. He died in London before he could return home. His son Moses later became Governor and was instrumental in Vermont's pursuit of statehood. Sherman et al, p. 81; Mello, pp. 36-37.

[23] *See* generally A.M. Caverly, *History of the Town of Pittsford, Vt.*

[24] One of these first cousins, Bailey Rawson, is honored by a monument in Rawsonville, Vermont, where the Rawson family gathers annually to celebrate the history of its forebears.

[25] Smith and Rann, pp. 726-48. Caverly describes Rawson's farm as being "bounded north by Peter Powers, east by John Fenn, south by Jacob Cooley, and west by Daniel Lee." Maps of the area from the late 1860s show the former Rawson property in the hands of John M Goodenough.

[26] Sherman et al, p. 161.

[27] As the British advanced south from Montreal, 106 Pittsford men traveled to Burlington and then crossed to Plattsburgh to help defend their country. Smith and Rann, p. 749.

[28] Klingaman and Klingaman, pp. 12, 13.

[29] Imbrie, pp. 181-83.

[30] *The Year Without a Summer*, www.vermonthistory.org.

[31] Klingaman and Klingaman, p. 197.

[32] Id., pp. 18-19.

[33] Sherman et al, pp. 172-73, 194.

[34] Id., p. 625 Appendix A.

[35] Sherman et al, p. 175. Looking further ahead as this exodus continued, the authors found that by the 1850 census, "[f]orty-two percent of all native-born Vermonters now resided outside the state." Id. at 210.

[36] David Hall was born in Bolton, Connecticut in 1762; he moved to Pittsford in 1803.

IV.
WEST TO MICHIGAN:
PITTSFORD TO MILAN

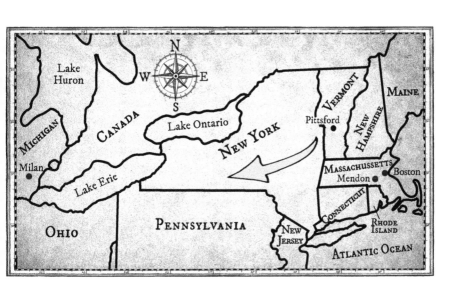

Ticket in hand, young Edward Rawson stood on the crowded wharf at Buffalo, New York, waiting for the call to board the steamboat that would carry him and his meager possessions the length of Lake Erie to Monroe, Michigan. He had spent the last five days on a succession of packet boats taking him and most of the others on the wharf from Albany to Buffalo on the busy Erie Canal. Much of the conversation during their slow progress along the canal was about the places people were headed: some to Ohio, many others to the territories called Michigan, Indiana and Wisconsin. The twenty-four year old from Pittsford, Vermont expected his relative, David Hall, to meet him at Monroe before traveling on together to the land they'd bought in Washtenaw County, twenty miles northwest of Monroe, near the southern border of the Michigan Territory. Like so many other New Englanders, the young men had been caught up in the excitement of the westward movement. Cheap land, accessible markets in the east for what they might grow, and the opportunity to find a wife and start a family must all have been part of what drew Edward west. Having lost his parents as a boy, Edward would have thought often about what it would be like to have a family of his own. But first he had to get himself to Michigan.

Finally the call rang out, "all aboard!"

Migration west to Michigan and the rest of what would be called the "Old Northwest" paralleled in many ways the movement of English settlers from Massachusetts and other areas into Vermont. There was the prospect of cheap land to settle and farm; there was a competing imperial power claiming hegemony; and there would be bloody wars fought over control of the region before widespread settlement by the new immigrants could begin.

As it did in Massachusetts and Vermont, however, the migration story of Michigan must start with the native tribes that settled there first. When the separate Iroquois tribes banded together in the Iroquois Confederation in the 1640s and subsequent decades, they fought the Algonquin and other tribes to expand their economic domination of the lands along the St. Lawrence, Lake Ontario and Lake Erie all the way to Lake Huron in the west. Among the many tribes pushed west by the Iroquois into what would become Ohio, Michigan and Indiana were the Shawnee, the Delaware and the Wyandot.

French explorers and fur traders had made their way into the Great Lakes lands from the north and east in the seventeenth century. Within ten years of Samuel de Champlain's founding of Montreal, Etienne Brule in 1618 explored west as far as the Sault St. Marie at the north end of Lake Michigan where it joins Lake Huron. Another Frenchman, Antoine de la Mouthe, founded a French trading post in 1701 at the location of future Detroit on the river just above the western end of Lake Erie. The English were slower than the French to start west but eventually came in far greater numbers from south of the Great Lakes. Traders and settlers moved west in Pennsylvania and Virginia and into the Ohio Valley in the decades from 1730 to 1760. A clash of these competing imperial powers was inevitable, and the local native tribes found themselves caught in the vice of the conflict—economic as well as military—just as they were in the northeast.

As described by historian R. Douglas Hurt, "[b]y the time tribal cultures arrived in Ohio... [t]he Native Americans were already dependent on European traders for the maintenance of a lifestyle that was no longer traditional. Indeed, they had lost much of their self-sufficiency."[1] The tribes became accustomed to hunting and fighting with guns instead of arrows, cooking with metal utensils and using manufactured axes and tools. They had also come to enjoy and expect "presents" from their European trading partners, who proved at various times that they did not understand the importance of these tokens in the reciprocity of relations expected by the Indians.

The Wyandots of northwest Ohio and southern Michigan aligned themselves with the French,[2] who had grown the Detroit trading post into a prominent settlement and fort. In contrast, the Shawnee and the Delaware to the south of Lake Erie in the Ohio River valley traded primarily with the British, although they were becoming very concerned with the increasing flow of settlers from Pennsylvania and Virginia who insisted on planting farms on native hunting grounds in the Ohio country. Again quoting Hurt, "by the early 1750s, both France and Great Britain realized that the political control of the [Indian] villages in the Ohio country would determine the imperial control of the North American continent."[3]

The war that ensued between the French and the British (with their Indian allies on each side) between 1754 and 1763 has been described earlier with its impact on migration in Massachusetts and Vermont. The conflict, now called the French and Indian War, was every bit as bloody in the Ohio country and surrounding lands. In 1752, a raiding party of French and their Indian allies devastated an English trading settlement at Pickawillany on the Miami River south of Lake Erie. In 1754, Virginia Major George Washington was defeated and forced to surrender Fort Necessity near the French Fort Duquesne in western Pennsylvania. As described in an earlier chapter, the subsequent invading force of British General Braddock and his redcoats in 1755 was routed by the French and Indians near the Monongahela River and future Pittsburgh. A British regiment lost badly again near Fort Duquesne in 1758 with hundreds of soldiers killed.[4] But the tide of the French and Indian War was about to turn under the firm hand of William Pitt back in London and the aggressive prosecution by his new commanding general for North America, Jeffrey Amherst.

In the Ohio country, the British convinced a number of France's Indian allies to switch sides in negotiations leading to the Treaty of Easton in 1758.[5] As a result of the changed balance of power, the French soon abandoned Fort Duquesne and retreated north to Michigan and Canada. When Montreal fell to the British in 1760 and the British navy scored victory after victory over France and Spain around the world, the war ended. The Treaty of Paris in 1763 ceded all of Canada, the Great Lakes country and the area east of the Mississippi River to the British. The fort at Detroit became a British outpost, though many French-Canadian settlers remained in the area.

The French had been defeated, but their Indian allies had not. Britain's Proclamation of 1763, which attempted to keep an uneasy peace with the natives by barring settlers from moving beyond the Appalachian Mountains and by creating an Indian "reserve," failed utterly as traders, hunters and farmers poured into the western lands. When crops failed and the tribes were beset with famine and disease, they got little help from their new British overlords.

To the contrary, the British insisted on the return of surviving captives from past attacks (many of whom had already been fully assimilated into their Indian captors' families), imposed limits on trade goods, cut back on granting presents and eased the way for yet more British settlers. This was too much for the Indians to suffer. A Delaware prophet named Neolin began to describe a vision he had been given by the "Maker of Heaven and Earth" of a return to the old native lifestyle, rejecting foreign powers and foreign ways (including alcohol and guns). In historian Hurt's words, Neolin provided "a spiritual nationalism that brought renewed violence to the Ohio country." The Ottawa chief Pontiac, whose tribe was centered in southern Michigan, proclaimed a clear and urgent goal for all of the tribes: "[T]hat we exterminate from our lands this nation which seeks only to destroy us."[6]

In the spring of 1763 an Indian revolution led by Pontiac and others threatened British traders, forts and settlers throughout the region. Pontiac moved on Fort Detroit and, when rebuffed, began a lengthy siege of the undermanned fort. At the same time, native warriors mounted attacks on smaller British forts at Sandusky, St. Joseph, Miami, Ouiatenon and Michilimackinac—an area stretching hundreds of miles from the south end of the Ohio River to the north end of Lake Huron. More than a thousand settlers were killed, as only the larger forts at Detroit, Pittsburgh and Niagara were successfully defended by the British. Pontiac eventually gave up the siege of Fort Detroit in the fall of 1763 after it had been reinforced with additional British troops. It took two more years for the British to mount the sustained counterattacks necessary to force peace on the Indian tribes, at least for a time. Colonel John Bradstreet and Colonel Henry Bouquet combined military force and hard bargaining to restore British control of the Ohio country. Pontiac's rebellion collapsed and he escaped to the Illinois country, where he met the same fate as Sassacus the Pequot sachem had in Massachusetts in 1637, killed by another tribe as he sought to escape.[7]

By the beginning of the Revolutionary War little more than a decade later, the Indian tribes greatly resented and felt threatened by the continued influx of settlers into their traditional lands. The British authorities did little to enforce the Proclamation of 1763, but they also did little to protect the settlers from the frequent raids of the natives in the Ohio country and elsewhere. With the advent of hostilities between the British and the Americans, in the words of Ron Chernow, "most tribes made the rational, if ultimately calamitous, decision that they had to protect their homelands and that the best way to do so was by supporting Great Britain, which they thought more likely to win the war."[8] Sometimes the natives supported His Majesty's redcoats in battle; at other times it was irregular bands of Tories and Indians who led murderous raids on American settlements in the frontier country of Pennsylvania and Virginia. Such attacks in the Wyoming Valley of Pennsylvania killed hundreds, leading Washington to order a "campaign of retribution and destruction" against more than forty Indian villages in the region.[9] Other bands used the British Fort Detroit to launch attacks against settlers in the Ohio country.

A critical counterstroke came when American Colonel George Rogers Clark moved in 1778 to eliminate several Indian villages and "to capture the bases from which the raiders struck." Clark attacked boldly against the British and their native allies in Indiana, capturing a British commander responsible for many of the raids and taking the important outpost at Vincennes. As historians have emphasized, Clark's success later enabled American peace negotiators in Paris to reject the British claim that the Ohio River rather than the Great Lakes should mark the northern boundary of United States territory[10]: "It was largely through Clark's efforts that the Northwest became part of the United States at the end of the Revolutionary War."[11]

In the years following the Revolutionary War, and as a result of lengthy and contentious negotiations, Virginia and then other states ceded their western lands to the new federal government. Needing cash, Congress wanted to facilitate sales of these lands, but first there needed to be a set of governing principles and processes for organizing the vast area. The Northwest Ordinance was approved in July 1787 to lay the necessary groundwork. When a district within the Northwest Territory (there were originally three) reached "a population of 5000 free males," it would gain a governor to be appointed by the Congress as well as an assembly for the territory. At 60,000 free males, the territory could become a state. The Ordinance also set out rules for surveying townships of thirty-six square miles each within a territory.[12] General Arthur St. Clair was named by Congress as the first territorial governor in 1788 and he remained in that role until 1802. Michigan qualified for separate territorial status in 1805, carved from the existing Indiana Territory two years after Ohio had become the first part of the original Northwest Territory to achieve statehood.

Land sales in the years following the Revolutionary War inevitably brought land speculation. Enormous tracts of land, encompassing millions of acres, were sold by the Congress and by the states in western and northern New York, northwest Pennsylvania, Maine, Georgia, and the Great Lakes country especially in Ohio. Speculators saw the opportunity for profit in taking their huge holdings, dividing them into smaller bundles and then selling them at higher prices as demand continued to increase. Some were able to use borrowed money and resell the properties even before their own payments came due. Others made improvements to the land (with roads or bridges) to enhance its value for sale.

Although speculators were often condemned as mere profiteers (who sometimes trafficked in bribes or fraud), many provided an important service to settlers by being willing to finance the purchases at a time when the government demanded cash payment and banks could be undependable lenders. As Kenneth E. Lewis describes, "the mortgage offered by the speculator was often the only source of capital available" on the frontier.[13] But speculation could and often did combine with legitimate demand to create financial bubbles which burst from time to time (as, for example, happened in 1792, 1796 and 1819).[14]

Settlers spilled west, but not without risk. For the thirty years between 1785 and 1815 the area that would become Michigan remained an attractive but dangerous arena in which Indians, British military and early American settlers would contend. Battles would be fought, treaties signed and ignored, and finally war would break out again between the young United States and the greatest military power on Earth—the British Empire.

The Peace of Paris ending the Revolutionary War in 1783 had left unclear the obligations of the British with respect to removal of their forces in disputed areas near the Great Lakes and the Mississippi Valley. Nor did the treaty address the status of natives living in the area north of the Ohio River. As the burgeoning swell of American settlers migrating west threatened to overrun Indian-claimed lands, the leaders of several tribes, including the Shawnees, Miamis, Wyandots and Ottawas, decided they would have to fight, and the British encouraged and supported the tribes in their "Northwest Indian War."

American settlers and militias fared poorly at first. After several losses by the poorly trained and badly led Americans, the

Revolutionary War hero General "Mad Anthony" Wayne assembled and drilled a professional fighting force of more than 2000 soldiers. At the Battle of Fallen Timbers on the Maumee River near what is now Toledo, the Americans routed a combined force of Indians and Canadian British.[15] Shortly after, in 1794, the Jay Treaty was signed requiring the British to "abandon all of their military posts on the American side of the Great Lakes."[16] This, in turn, led to the 1795 Treaty of Grenville between the Americans and a number of tribal leaders, turning over a huge swath of Indian land to the American government. Settlers renewed their rush into the area.

Conflict between the encroaching settlers and the displaced tribes escalated. More battles were followed by more treaties opening the way for more settlers. As aptly described by historian Frederick Merk: "Throughout American history treaties with Indians have taken effect only against Indians, for the frontier could never be brought to respect such treaties."[17] The Treaty of Detroit in 1807 gave the Americans claim to all of southern Michigan. The Treaty of Fort Wayne in 1809 ceded lands in central and western Indiana. In the words of Samuel Eliot Morison, "American policy toward the natives of North America... continued an old world process of one race or people pushing a weaker one out of an area that it wanted."[18]

By 1810, a Shawnee chief named Tecumseh had seen enough. He and his brother, known as the Prophet, tried to unite several tribes in a war to drive back the ever increasing numbers of white settlers. But while Tecumseh was away in the south trying to convince the Cherokees to join his war, General William Henry Harrison attacked and destroyed a Shawnee village called "Prophetstown" for Tecumseh's brother. History would call this engagement something else, the Battle of Tippecanoe, and its consequences would be enormous. As described by Walter Borneman, an enraged Tecumseh would throw himself into the arms of the British to seek vengeance even as political opinion in the United States, especially in the west, turned strongly toward war with Great Britain.[19] (In the longer term, of course, the Battle of Tippecanoe would ring in the short-lived presidency of General Harrison with the 1840 campaign cry of "Tippecanoe and Tyler, Too.")

With Henry Clay leading the western war hawks in Congress, the United States responded to a number of provocations on the high seas by declaring war against Great Britain. The War of 1812 (which lasted until 1815) had several theaters of operation, including Atlantic naval engagements, the Lake Champlain corridor (as described in the earlier chapter on Vermont), the upper Chesapeake Bay attacks on Washington, D.C. and Baltimore, and at the mouth of the Mississippi at New Orleans. But the theater of war that most affected Michigan and the west encompassed the Great Lakes.

When war was declared, American land forces were thinly spread in northern Ohio and southern Michigan, with a tenuous hold on forts at Mackinaw Island, Detroit and Chicago. British naval forces, though light, were sufficient to control western Lake Erie and to support British troops in upper Canada across the river from Detroit. A small number of British ships also managed to control Lakes Huron and Michigan.

The American fort at Mackinaw Island at the top of Michigan was the first to fall. Next, American forces at Fort Detroit under General William Hull were surrounded by the British and their Indian allies in August of 1812. Without any prospect of reinforcements, and after only a brief bombardment of the fort, Hull surrendered his 2500 man force, hoping to avoid a post-battle massacre. When the Americans also surrendered Fort Dearborn (Chicago), they were not so lucky. Retreating American troops were ambushed by Potawatomi fighters and scores were tomahawked and scalped.

Worse was yet to come. As General Hull was removed and shipped back east to face court martial for too easily abandoning Fort Detroit, General Harrison made plans to retake the fort. He sent a force of Kentucky militia men north under General James Winchester to establish a camp on the Maumee River in January of 1813 and to prepare for a move on Detroit and Canada. Winchester, however, saw an opportunity to advance into Michigan and imprudently took it. At Frenchtown on the River Raisin (modern Monroe, Michigan), the Americans successfully drove away a small combined British and Indian force. But the British soon reinforced their numbers and counterattacked the stunningly unprepared Americans. Almost a thousand Americans were killed or captured at this second Battle of Frenchtown. Scores more were massacred after the battle as they fled. The Americans suffered additional losses of more than 600 at the British and Indian siege of Fort Meigs in Ohio in April 1813, although Harrison held the fort and the invaders eventually withdrew. A second British attempt on Fort Meigs in July was again repulsed and an attack on the well-defended Fort Stephenson near Sandusky failed as well after a fierce battle.[20] As summer turned into fall in 1813, the British and their native allies led by Tecumseh held the upper hand in the western theater. But that was about to change.

The American naval captain (later commodore) Oliver Hazard Perry became the hero of the war in the west in September of 1813. Both sides recognized that control of Lake Erie to enable transport of troops and materiel by ship would be the key to victory in the region. The British under Commander Robert H. Barclay launched an ambitious ship-building project at Amherstberg on the Canadian side of the lake near Detroit, while the Americans under Perry hurried to use Presque Isle Bay near Erie, Pennsylvania to construct their fleet.

Both sides finished their work at about the same time, and Perry (after a difficult and vulnerable time getting his newly-built ships successfully over the sand bars that protected the bay) headed west to find the British fleet. He stopped at Put-in-Bay in the Lake Erie Islands near Sandusky to gather intelligence about the British and to finalize his plan of attack. Barclay, meanwhile, chose an offensive strategy; the British fleet made its way from Amherstburg southeast toward the islands, hoping to put the Americans at a disadvantage. His hand forced, Perry had to fight adverse winds leaving his anchorage at Put-in-Bay, his ships tacking back and forth to clear Rattlesnake Island even as the British approached.

But Perry was a lucky man, as the wind shifted unexpect-
edly to his advantage, enabling him to approach the British at
an angle keeping him out of range of the British long guns until
the Americans were close enough to engage. The two sides set up
their line of battle and the competing flagships, the *Detroit* under
Barclay and the *Lawrence* under Perry, opened fire, hammering
at each other for more than two hours of devastating cannon-
ades. With the *Lawrence* practically disabled, its decks slippery
with blood, Perry abandoned his command vessel and was rowed
to the Americans' second largest ship, the *Niagara*, which had
been late to engage but now positioned itself for action. Barclay's
Detroit had also been badly damaged and, under withering fire
from the *Niagara*, the British commander was eventually forced
to strike his colors and surrender the fleet. The triumphant Perry
sent to General Harrison his historic message: "We have met the
enemy and they are ours."[21]

Control of Lake Erie now assured, the Americans once
again advanced on Canada. With Perry's ships transporting
Harrison's army, the Americans moved north from Ohio along
Lake Erie to retake Detroit and prepare to invade British Upper
Canada, now dangerously isolated in the west. Crossing the
Detroit River into Canada with a strong force of 3000, General
Harrison engaged and defeated a smaller British and Indian force
at Thames, Ontario. One of those who fell in the battle was the
Shawnee chief Tecumseh, depriving the warring tribes of their
most aggressive and effective leader. As historian R. Douglas Hurt
put it, "the Battle of the Thames… had broken British power in
the Northwest and destroyed Tecumseh's Indian confederacy."[22]
When the War of 1812 ended with the peace treaty of Ghent,
and yet another Indian treaty imposed the will of the Americans
on the natives in 1815, Michigan and Ohio as well as the rest of
the Northwest was ready for renewed settlement.

Little time was wasted in preparing the lands for settlers.
The federal government conducted surveys beginning in 1816,
and public sales began in 1818.[23] Historian Morison describes the
attractiveness of the new lands: "A favorite objective for Yankee

settlement was southern Michigan, a rolling country of 'oak openings,' where stately trees stood well-spaced as in a park."[24] Pioneers quickly recognized the advantage of these oak openings over the marshy lands closer to the lakefront as well as the heavily timbered areas that would require so much more labor. Clearing the openings, in the words of Michigan historian Kenneth E. Lewis, "usually involved girdling the trees, removing those necessary for fencing, burning the debris and brush, and plowing."[25] Once prepared, these areas were ideal for cultivating not only subsistence crops but also the principal cash crop, wheat.

Speculators played a role in the settling of Michigan, as elsewhere, but a number of the newcomers who came west had sold property back in the northeast for many times what they would need to pay in Michigan. New England land could sell for $20 or $30 per acre while the government offered new lands in the west for just $1.25.[26] Of course, there was more involved in starting a farm than just the cost of the land. Land had to be cleared, plowed and planted; houses and barns had to be built; equipment had to be purchased. The start up costs for an 80 acre farm in Michigan in the 1820s or 1830s have been estimated at about $1500.[27] Waves of immigrants were undaunted.

Lewis describes well the drivers of this mass movement from east to west: "Changing economic conditions on the Eastern Seaboard induced emigration. Rapid population growth, from natural increase and European immigration, placed increasing pressure on limited land resources. Traditional farming became increasingly unprofitable because of higher operating cost, increased land values, competition from western agriculture, and often declining output from worn-out lands. Although many eastern farmers found employment in manufacturing, others looked toward resettlement in the West as a solution to these conditions." [28]

But how would all these new settlers get to the west from New York and New England?

When historians of migration describe the key factors that drive the process of migration to new lands, as described earlier, they talk about *pull, push* and *means*: what attracts settlers to a new place; what drives them away from an old place; and how they can get from the old to the new. There are probably no better examples of the means factor than the impact the Erie Canal and steamship navigation had on the peopling of the upper Middle West early in the nineteenth century after the British and the Indian threats had been eliminated.

The Erie Canal was the most prominent and the most successful product of the canal-building movement that began in the years after the United States won its independence. George Washington recognized the importance of finding cheap transportation routes past the low mountains and ridge lines of the Appalachians. He longed to make the Potomac River the main artery of commerce from the interior, and spent years leading and supporting the effort to build a canal and locks from the Potomac above Georgetown to newly settled areas of Pennsylvania and western Virginia. Washington didn't live to see his treasured "Patowmack Canal" project completed, as it began service two years after his death in 1799, never made money and ceased commercial operations by 1830.

To the north, New York Governor De Witt Clinton had the same dream but a better topographical path to its achievement. The Hudson River is fully navigable north to Albany, where it is entered by the east flowing Mohawk River. Although the Mohawk tumbles east through a gorge not far from Albany, it mostly runs through relatively flat terrain across central New York. Clinton recognized that a canal and locks could provide a water route all the way to Lake Erie near Buffalo, where goods could be loaded on or unloaded from ships making regular trips along the Ohio and Michigan coasts to growing port cities in Cleveland, Sandusky and Detroit. It would also greatly increase the value of farmlands across New York state.

As described by Peter Bernstein in *Wedding of the Waters*, it was the War of 1812 that "revealed the tragic lack of adequate transportation facilities to link the lands around Lake Erie with the east."[29] Clinton overcame substantial political obstacles to the project by arguing, in part, that a waterway between the lakes and the Hudson would not only reduce the cost of commercial shipments but also help the fledgling nation to bind the growing west to the settled east, politically as well as economically. After several false starts and disappointments, the project got underway on July 4, 1817, its entire expense of more than $6 million funded by New York state and private investors rather than the federal government.

In a world of power excavation, dynamite, concrete and steel rebar, it is hard to imagine the human effort required to dig Governor Clinton's big ditch. The canal needed to be forty feet wide and four feet deep, with tow paths carved on either side for mules or horses. It covered 363 miles from Albany to Buffalo, and required the construction of 83 locks, each 90 feet long and 15 feet wide, to lift or lower canal boats 8 feet 4 inches in each lock. Thousands of men worked for more than 8 years to connect the various segments of the project, which included 18 tall aqueducts to carry canal boats over parts of the Genesee and Mohawk rivers. Finally, in an emotional trip from Lake Erie to Albany and then down the Hudson to New York City in October 1825, Governor Clinton celebrated the opening of the canal by dramatically pouring a cask filled with Lake Erie water into the Atlantic Ocean outside New York harbor. The Erie Canal was open for business.[30]

Within the first year, 7000 boats were operating on the canal.[31] In the words of historian Frederick Merk, the canal "proved an immediate success, reducing the costs of shipping grain between Buffalo and New York City from $100 to $15 a ton, and travel time from 20 days to 8."[32] But the canal did much more than carry grain from western fields to eastern markets. It also facilitated the growing movement, mostly of families, who were leaving farms and factories in New England and elsewhere for the Old Northwest Territory. Passenger boats could travel the canal in as little as five days. As Bernstein put it, the Erie Canal "carried almost all the people moving out to Ohio and then on to the Great Lakes."[33] No longer would it be necessary to spend weeks on foot, on horseback

or in a Conestoga wagon[34] to cross the Alleghenies into newly
opened lands. The canal changed all that.

The canal, yes, but also the steamboats that met the canal in
the fast growing port city of Buffalo. Steamship navigation was the
second great means factor of migration to the upper Middle West.

Steam was harnessed as a practical source of power by James
Watt in England around 1775. An American, Robert Fulton of
New York, traveled in Europe between 1786 and 1806 and wit-
nessed the different uses of steam engines. John Fitch first dem-
onstrated on the Delaware River in 1787 that a steam engine
could be used to power a boat. But it was Fulton and his partner,
the Hudson Valley scion Robert Livingston, who showed that
a steamboat could provide regular, reliable commercial service.
Their *Clermont* (first called the *North Shore Steamboat* when
launched in 1807) covered the 150 miles from New York City
to Albany up the Hudson River in 32 hours. Fulton also dem-
onstrated that steamboats could operate safely on the Ohio and
Mississippi Rivers all the way to New Orleans.[35] The "second
steamship in the world to operate on a regular schedule" was the
Vermont, on Lake Champlain. Importantly, the 120 foot *Vermont*
"proved that steamboats could operate in open waters and against
adverse winds and large waves," a critical step on the larger and
rougher waters of the Great Lakes.[36]

After the War of 1812, water transport on Lake Erie was provided by a collection of wind-powered sailing ships, largely sloops
and schooners, although small open boats were often needed to
load or offload cargo in the meager harbors along the Ohio and
Michigan coast. The alternative, stagecoach travel along the south
or the north sides of Lake Erie, was longer, slower and less comfortable than the water route. The stage route from Buffalo to
Detroit rode 375 hard miles along the south side; it was nearly 300
on the Canadian side of the lake but with fewer populated areas
for services. In winter, of course, the land route was the only choice.

As the Erie Canal project was just getting started, the first
steamboat on Lake Erie, the *Walk-in-the-Water*, was launched near
Buffalo in 1818. A second, the *Superior*, began to provide round

trip service to Detroit in 1822, and a third, the *Niagara*, had its maiden voyage in 1826. Soon the lake was filled with steamboats, competing for business with the many sailing ships. The *Michigan Gazetteer* reported there were more than 50 steamboats and more than 200 sloops and schooners plying Lake Erie in 1838. Cabin passage on a steamboat from Buffalo to Detroit cost $8 and the trip took only two and a half to five days; sailing ships cost less, but the passage took much longer, often up to nine days.[37]

An article in the *Toledo Blade* newspaper early in 1838 detailed the lake traffic into the western Lake Erie port of Toledo (a stopping point from Buffalo on the way to Detroit). In 1836, steamboats made 330 stops, and schooners 271. Just one year later, the numbers had increased to 756 steamboat stops and 203 schooners. This was in addition to frequent small steamboat traffic between Toledo and Detroit.[38] All of this lake traffic took place between around April 1, when the winter ice would usually have broken up, to December 1, by which time the lake often froze back over.[39]

The opening of the Erie Canal and the advent of steam navigation contributed to a great surge of migration into Michigan in the first half of the nineteenth century. In 1810, the territory's population was just 4,528. That number nearly doubled after the War of 1812, to 9,048 in 1820. But the Erie Canal and the Lake Erie steamships helped the population to triple to 32,538 by 1830, and the floodgates had only just opened. By 1834 the population of Michigan had increased to 87,278. And by the end of 1837, more than 175,000 settlers had made Michigan their home. In Detroit alone in 1831, according to Kenneth E. Lewis, "[a]n estimated two thousand persons per week arrived... double the number of two years earlier." More than two-thirds of the immigrants made their way from New England or New York; the other third came up through Ohio from Virginia and the mid-Atlantic region or down from Canada.[40]

The sharp economic downturn of the Panic of 1837 (caused by President Jackson's war against the Bank of the United States and the resulting collapse in credit, so vital to land speculation) marked the end of this early wave of migration into Michigan, only to be resumed in the 1840s and later.

Having exceeded the 60,000 free white males threshold of the Northwest Ordinance, Michigan was admitted to the Union in 1837 as the twenty-sixth state. But its path to admission was not straight, because the territory's southern border was not straight. And, as with Vermont fifty years earlier, Michigan's entry was essentially held hostage by a strong state until land disputes were satisfactorily resolved. This episode is often referred to as the "Toledo War," because the land in dispute between Michigan and Ohio included the valuable mouth of the Maumee River at Lake Erie where Toledo sits.

The problem began with territorial surveys conducted pursuant to the Northwest Ordinance of 1787. Surveyors drew a line from the south end of Lake Michigan across the Michigan peninsula to Lake Erie, and this was the border recognized when Ohio became a state in 1803. Only later was it recognized that the maps used as the basis for the survey had put the south end of Lake Michigan too far north, giving Ohio land that should have been in the Michigan Territory. Why did it matter, beyond the obvious question of land sales and claims (although some of the land was the miserable Great Black Swamp surrounding the Maumee River)? Because Ohio canal builders planned to use the Maumee Bay as the entry port to Lake Erie from the interior of Ohio and Indiana, but the river mouth and bay now appeared to be inside the area claimed by Michigan. Ohio had even begun to build a new port town, Toledo, at the contested location. When new, federally mandated surveys were conducted in 1817 and 1818, it became clear that strict compliance with the Northwest Ordinance would give a strip of land from the Indiana border to Lake Erie to Michigan, not Ohio. Eight miles wide at its eastern end and containing 468 square miles of land, the "Toledo Strip" included all of Maumee Bay and Toledo. Ohioans were incensed.

All of the political power lay with Ohio, which was already a well-populated member of the federal Union. But Michigan did not back down. When Ohio sent surveying teams into the strip, Michigan officials had them arrested (just as Vermont officials had done to New York surveyors in the New Hampshire Grants in 1775) and sent its militia into the disputed lands. Shots were fired and tempers flared. Ohio, however, held the trump card as Michigan was seeking Congressional approval of its admission to the Union in 1833. Eventually, Michigan was offered and accepted the three-quarters of the Upper Peninsula that up to that time had been part of the Wisconsin territory; in return, Michigan ceded to Ohio its claims to the "Toledo Strip." Congress then approved Michigan's statehood application, and Michigan was admitted to the Union in January 1837. So ended the Toledo War.[41]

Early migration from the east had focused on Detroit as the port of entry from which settlers advanced northwest and southeast. Between 1819 and 1823, however, immigrants discovered the attractions of the area west of Monroe, forty miles south of Detroit. A second federal land office was set up in Monroe, whose attractive natural harbor was already a stopping point for lake traffic headed to Detroit and Monroe soon became "Michigan's second-most-important commercial port."[42] This and other parts of Michigan exemplified what historians call "agricultural colonization," the process by which settlers are drawn to a landscape because of its potential for productive commercial agriculture, not just family-based subsistence farming. By 1840 Washtenaw County, situated west of Monroe, had become one of the largest wheat-producing areas in Michigan,[43] filling wagons which stopped to transfer their loads into Monroe warehouses from which the grain would be loaded onto ships headed back east across Lake Erie.

✳ ✳ ✳ ✳

Edward Rawson, the orphan from Pittsford, Vermont, joined the wave of migration to cheap new lands in Michigan in 1835, when he was 24 years old. The land he bought was in London Township, Washtenaw County, in southern Michigan, eighty acres in September and another eighty acre plot in October at the standard government price of $1.25

an acre. He met and married another eastern emigrant, Sarah
Newell Spalding, two years later. She was the daughter of John
Spalding and Anna Kingsley, who had left Fort Ann in upstate
New York for the Michigan Territory in 1832 after John pur-
chased 400 acres of attractive southern Michigan farmland in
1831 and 1832.[44]

The township of Milan (pronounced "my´-len" rather than
"mill-ahn´") was carved from London township in 1836 (Milan
is split between Washtenaw County and Monroe County), and
Edward Rawson's father-in-law John Spalding became first a justice of the peace and later a town supervisor in 1842. Michigan
settlers had to contend with fierce winter weather in 1831, again
in 1836-37, and a third time in 1842–43.[45] The Vermont orphan
Edward Rawson's chapter in the Rawson migration tale is a
short one, as he died in 1847 at the age of 35.[46] But the family's
Michigan roots deepened as his son, John Spalding Rawson, and
then three more generations of descendants remained in the same
part of southern Michigan.[47]

The unabashedly promotional 1838 *"Gazetteer of the State of
Michigan"* concluded with a bit of advice for prospective immigrants. The admonition rings true for all of the two hundred years
of migrations recounted here, and so is worth quoting at length:

> *"If there are any who have regretted the change, it is from
> causes, arising either from casualty, their own improvidence, or
> an injudicious selection of a location. It is true, individuals may
> be found who are disaffected. But these are to be found in every
> county and in every community. Disaffection is an innate disorder
> — a natural deformity of the mind of some persons. These are eas-
> ily persuaded to emigrate because they cannot be contented. They
> begin to search for the philosopher's stone in a westward paradise.
> They commence a westward progression without a fixed point of
> settlement or termination of travel. They will pass through the
> most delightful regions of nature without the thought of locating
> short of the 'far west.' At last they reach the occident of emigration,
> the western frontier, and finally conclude to make a settlement.*

Such persons will rarely make a satisfactory choice. Every breeze of rumor chants the praises of other locations. They change and change until persuaded they have gone too far. Their own folly begets disgust, and, if they retire, they return impoverished, casting imprecations upon the country... Everyone proposing to emigrate would do well first to have a definite conception in his own mind what his wants are.[8]

Many emigrants did not know their own minds or wants. Some, however—like the Rawsons of Michigan—did. They had made a satisfactory choice to settle in southern Michigan, without regrets or disaffection, and there they stayed, generation after generation, for more than a hundred years.

---

[1] Hurt, p. 31 et seq.

[2] Wright, pp. 12–14.

[3] Hurt, p. 38.

[4] Borneman, pp. 160–61.

[5] Id., pp. 162–64.

[6] Hurt, pp. 40–47 et seq.; Brown, p. 4; Wright, p. 110. As observed by Alexis de Toqueville, there may have been a time when united native tribes could have driven the earliest settlers back to Europe. *Discovery in America*, Vol I, p. 342 and n. 10. Pontiac came a century too late to succeed at that.

[7] Hurt, pp. 48–54; Borneman, pp. 283–304; Merk, pp. 65–66.

[8] Chernow, *Washington*, p. 359

[9] Allen, *Tories*, pp. 256, 263–65; Bobrick, *Angel in the Whirlwind*, pp. 374–76.

[10] Allen, pp. 274–75; Bobrick, pp. 376–77.

[11] Fischer and Kelly, p. 168.

[12] Morison, *American People*, pp. 300–01. In Morison's view, "no more important enactment was ever made by the Confederation."

[13] Lewis, p. 110.

[14] Merk, pp. 112–118.

[15] Chernow (*Washington* at p. 717) says that the Battle of Fallen

Timbers "broke the back of Indian power in the region and ended British influence with the dominant tribes."

[16] Borneman, p. 27.

[17] Merk, p. 69.

[18] Morison, p. 445.

[19] Id. at p. 37.

[20] Hurt, pp. 333–40.

[21] Perry had named his flagship the USS *Lawrence* in memory of his friend Captain James Lawrence, who died in battle on the USS *Chesapeake* after giving the immortal order "Don't Give Up The Ship." Perry had the motto emblazoned on a banner and flown over the *Lawrence*. Ironically, Perry contradicted his friend's motto, gave up his ship and won the battle as a result.

[22] *See* generally http://geo.msu.edu; Hurt, p. 342.

[23] Blois, *Michigan Gazeteer*, p. 195.

[24] Morison, p. 475.

[25] Lewis, p. 56.

[26] Merk, p. 116.

[27] Lewis, p. 106.

[28] Id. at p. 128.

[29] Bernstein, p. 175.

[30] Id., pp. 26, 180, 191, 208, 231, 318–19.

[31] Id., p. 325.

[32] Merk, p. 217.

[33] Bernstein, p. 350.

[34] Although the Conestoga wagon is often (and incorrectly) referred to as the great "prairie schooner" of the Great Plains and the Oregon Trail later in the 19th century, the wagon had its origin in Conestoga, Pennsylvania, where German (or "Pennsylvania Deutsch") craftsmen adapted European style wagons to American needs. It was the preferred transport for migrants heading to the Old Northwest until displaced (where feasible) by canal boats and steamships. *See* Merk, p. 50. Later settlers heading to the far west relied on wagons that were smaller and lighter than the Conestogas.

[35] Demonstrating the close connection between the Erie Canal and steamship travel, Robert Fulton served on New York State's Erie

Canal Commission from 1811 until his death. Fulton is buried in the cemetery of Trinity Church in lower Manhattan, just a few yards from the grave of Alexander Hamilton.

[36] Sherman et al, p. 149.

[37] Blois, p. 415; Lewis, pp. 24–25.

[38] Waggoner, p. 454.

[39] Id., p. 102.

[40] Blois, pp. 150, 157; Lewis, p. 223.

[41] *See* generally http://geo.msu.edu and http://www.michigan. gov/dmva; Lewis, p. 100. There is an interesting modern postscript to the Toledo War. Michigan and Ohio continued for over 130 years to dispute possession of the small, uninhabited Turtle Island, the westernmost of the Lake Erie Islands. In 1973, an agreement was reached to draw the boundary line between the states right down the middle of Turtle Island, with the Michigan side made part of Erie Township and the Ohio side part of the city of Toledo. The author recalls visiting the island by boat around 1960 with his grandparents Joseph and Eleanor Reiter from their lakefront home in Luna Pier, Michigan near Erie.

[42] Lewis, p. 203.

[43] Id., at pp. 1–2, 245.

[44] A sister of Sarah Newell Spalding, named Laurena, also married an emigrant from Rutland County, Vermont; his name was D.P. Potter and he settled in nearby Monroe, Michigan in 1842.

[45] Lewis, p. 65.

[46] Edward Rawson's grave is marked by a still legible stone in the Spaulding Cemetery in Milan, Michigan. Other Rawsons and Spauldings are also buried there.

[47] Edward Rawson's daughter, Rosina, born in 1846 just a year before her father died, married Jesse Redman of Milan in 1866.

[48] Blois, p. 416.

EPILOGUE

The discovery of gold at Sutter's Mill in the California territory in 1848 drew men (and some women) from every corner of the country. So did the Oklahoma land rush in 1889. But the Rawsons of Milan, Michigan were not among those who sold everything to chase the dream of easy wealth in the west, those who searched "for the philosopher's stone in a westward paradise." They ignored the siren song of the great gold rush. They resisted the allure of cheap new land in the territories beyond Illinois and Kansas and Nebraska. They put down deep roots right there in the rich soil of the southern Michigan farmlands, generation after generation after generation. The tides of migration washed around and past them but did not catch them up.

The Civil War came and went. Reconstruction in the South and the Great Migration northward of free blacks never changed the small towns between Toledo and Detroit the way they did those and many other northern cities. Henry Ford's automobile assembly plants in Dearborn and elsewhere made for jobs and a growing Michigan economy in the first part of the twentieth century. When the stock market crashed and the Great Depression settled on the land, most in the area did their best just to hold on, with the help of neighbors and friends. But the Second World War opened the eyes of many young men from these small towns to the greater world outside, drawing them into uniforms and assignments far away. And after the war's end the GI Bill gave some of those same young men a path out of their small towns and into new places and ways.

American migration no longer ran primarily east to west or south to north. Education brought opportunity, and opportunity grew large after the war, especially near the revitalized urban centers of the east. The great twentieth century technology companies like General Electric, IBM and AT&T filled their headquarters and research laboratories with bright, ambitious, upwardly mobile college graduates. They came not just from the

ivy-covered campuses of the northeast but also from state universities and land grant colleges across the nation.

One of the bright young men willing to pick up and seek his
fortune in the new technology melting pot back east was Harold
Rawson of Temperance, Michigan, a tenth generation descendant
of Secretary Edward Rawson. The GI Bill and a lot of hard work
earned him a degree as an electrical engineer from the University
of Toledo in 1950. After marrying his college sweetheart, Joyce
Reiter of Toledo, and taking a job with AT&T's Western Electric
company, he moved with her to New York City, then Newark, and
finally to Florham Park in the fast growing suburbs of northern
New Jersey.

Significantly, for the first time in his long line of migrating
Rawson forebears, Hal Rawson made a move that was untethered
to any family connection. When Secretary Edward Rawson came
to Massachusetts Bay from England in the 1630s, he followed
his uncle the Rev. John Wilson. When William Rawson moved
to Mendon, Massachusetts, he was preceded by his prominent
uncle the Rev. Grindal Rawson. When Leonard Rawson moved
to Vermont in 1800, he traveled a path already taken by a number
of his Mendon cousins. And when young Edward Rawson made
the long journey to Michigan in 1835, he bought land together
with a family relative who had already settled there. Hal and Joyce
Rawson, in contrast, left family and friends behind in the mid-
west to make their own way back east, eventually finding suburban Florham Park in 1956.

Suburbs have often been denigrated in modern American
culture. The stereotypical image is a sprawling post-WWII
Levittown in New York, Pennsylvania or New Jersey, with affordable cookie cutter houses on small lots in giant developments.
One writer, John C. Teaford, has captured the caricature view
of these places: "[A] bland, homogeneous zone producing dull
drones in look-alike houses... wreaking havoc with civilization
and nature." Immediately debunking this one-sided perspective,
however, Teaford went on to point out that "model suburban
neighborhoods" have been around since the 1870s; that suburbs

have always reflected a wide diversity of purposes and ways of living; and that "[t]he American suburb is a prime example of the
nation's tradition of expansive freedom and mobility."[1]

Florham Park, New Jersey in the 1950s and 1960s represented the best of the suburban experience. Settled in 1715 as
a farming community, Florham Park was close enough to New
York City and Newark to provide convenient and comfortable
homes not only for those employed nearby but also for commut-
ers to the job-rich cities, benefiting from accessible highways and
nearby rail transportation. When large companies began to move
their operations and even their headquarters away from the cities
and into regional centers, Florham Park was ideally situated. In
addition to affordable and attractive housing, Florham Park provided progressive local government, excellent public and private
schools, and ample open spaces and recreational opportunities
for young families. All of this contributed to a strong sense of
civic pride in its citizens, shown to this day by the Fourth of July
parade and related celebrations that bring many former residents
back to reconnect with old friends. It was a place, in short, for
people to put down roots—deep, strong and lasting.[2]

In the next generation after Harold and Joyce Rawson[3] settled in Florham Park, all four of their adult children remained in
or returned to within 25 miles of the town. Of their eleven grown
grandchildren, seven have continued to live nearby. But the forces
of migration, particularly the pull of economic opportunity in
a mobile world, remain strong. One grandson moved to North
Carolina for college, marriage and a career. A second has been
drawn to New York City by the attractions of an urban lifestyle
and profession. Another made his way to the beautiful Rocky
Mountains of Colorado. And, in a bit of historical irony, one
has gone full circle, returning to the Boston area that Secretary
Edward Rawson called home more than three hundred and seventy years ago.

Now another generation in this line of Rawsons—the thirteenth since Secretary Edward Rawson—has entered the scene.
There's no way to know where they will settle or migrate to, or

what may pull or push them to different places. The new chapter they have opened in this ongoing Rawson family migration story remains to be written. But at least they will understand where they've come from, who has gone before them, and why their forebears migrated from Gillingham to Boston, from Mendon to Pittsford, and from Milan to Florham Park.

This new generation will bear watching, indeed!

---

[1] See *The American Suburb* by John C. Teaford, at pp. xiii, 1, 7, 217–19. Professor Witold Rybczynski cites in his *City Life* (p. 175) the work of other historians demonstrating that, far from being a recent development, some of the earliest American suburbs date to 1814 around New York, 1820 near Boston, and the 1840s outside Philadelphia.

[2] Harold and Joyce Rawson and others who moved into Florham Park and similar suburban areas were in good company. As Theodore White described in his momentous *The Making of the President 1960*, the growth of the suburbs between 1950 and 1960 accounted for two-thirds of the 28,000,000 increase in the American population in the decade and profoundly changed "the American pattern of living" (pp. 217–18).

[3] The significant contributions of Joyce Rawson, both as a volunteer active in many organizations and as "one of the most knowledgeable people the Borough has ever employed," are noted in *Saga of A Crossroads: Florham Park* by Eleanor Weis. *See* pp. 158, 172, 182.

APPENDIX ONE

A RAWSON LINEAGE FROM 1615 TO 2002[1]

E dward Rawson, who was born in Gillingham, England in
1615 and migrated to Massachusetts around 1636, is considered the progenitor of nearly all of those bearing the
Rawson name in the United States. He has been characterized
as "part of a small number of elites who came from England" to
become the "Puritan upper class in New England."[2] His grandfather, also named Edward, was a propertied merchant of silks and
woolens, and his father, David Rawson, has been described as a
merchant tailor from London, well-connected to business and
Puritan religious leaders in England. Edward's mother, Margaret
Wilson, was the sister of the Rev. John Wilson, who accompanied John Winthrop to Massachusetts in 1630 and who founded
the First Church in Boston. This latter connection is likely a
principal reason for Edward's migration to the Colony. Another
of his mother's brothers, Edmond Wilson, provided substantial
financial support to the Puritan immigrants in New England.[3]

Edward married Rachel Perne in England in 1636 and the
couple had a daughter there (an infant they left behind) before
they boarded ship for America. Like her husband, Rachel came
from a well-to-do family near Gillingham. Her parents, Richard
and Rachel (Greene) Perne, leased a substantial house called East
Haimes,[4] a traditional perquisite of the "Fee Forester" responsible
for the Gillingham royal forest; although the land had not been
used as a royal forest for many years, the area remained the property of King Charles I. (As described in an earlier note, Rachel
(Perne) Rawson's family back in England endured trying times
during the English Civil War as the forest-related uprisings
swept the area.)

Arriving in New England, Edward and Rachel settled in Newbury, founded in 1634 north of Boston. That Edward was well off is shown by the fact that he brought to the colony with him at least one servant, a man named Richard Crane. Despite his young age (just 21 or 22 when he arrived), Edward quickly rose to prominence in Newbury. He was appointed to committees concerning the apportionment of grazing land; the appraisal of livestock for tax assessments; the management of the town's affairs; and the compilation of the town's laws. He became the Town Clerk in 1638, receiving praise that "the records are fuller and more comprehensive, and dates are given with more regularity and exactness" since his appointment as clerk. He was entrusted with the role of "tax farmer" to collect excise taxes due on the sale of wine and "strong water," and was awarded a contract to manufacture gunpowder for the town.[5]

After his election to the House of Deputies for the Colony, Edward became Secretary of that body and a few years later, in 1650, Secretary of the Great and General Court, a position he maintained through annual elections until 1686, when the government of the Colony was taken over and its leadership replaced for a time by the royalist Sir Edmund Andros.

Secretary Rawson shouldered the responsibility for keeping the records of the General Court, signing orders and maintaining the law rolls. He also served on various committees of the General Court. These were tempestuous times for the colonials. During his thirty-six years in office, Secretary Rawson's signature appeared on orders of the General Court concerning the creation of new settlements or "plantations" (including the incorporation of Mendon); the defense of the colony during the bloody King Philip's War and the "Thanksgiving Proclamation" near its conclusion; the fierce persecution of the Quakers; and the often troubled relations with royal authorities back in England. He also signed warrants for the arrests of two of "the regicides," English judges who had been involved in the imprisonment and execution of King Charles I but who had escaped to the colony to avoid retribution from Charles II (they eluded arrest there as well).

Secretary Rawson received several land grants as part of his compensation over the years; the *Rawson Family Memoir* (p. 258) estimates that he held over 6,000 acres of land. One such award was a grant of 2,000 acres in 1685 in Mendon, where his son, Grindal, had settled after being called as minister in 1680. Secretary Rawson later transferred 800 acres of his Mendon land to another son, Grindal's older brother, William.

A member for many years at the First Church during the ministry of his uncle, the Rev. John Wilson, Secretary Rawson was one of a group of twenty-eight disaffected parishioners who left the church after Rev. Wilson's death to form the Third Church in 1669, also called the Old South Church.[6] Secretary Rawson was well-connected to the clergy in England as well as in Boston. His maternal grandfather, Rev. William Wilson, was a chaplain to the Archbishop of Canterbury, Rev. Edmund Grindal, and his maternal grandmother, Isabell (Woodhull) Wilson, was a niece of that Archbishop. Secretary Rawson's wife, Rachel (Perne) Rawson, also had clerical connections as she was related through her maternal grandfather, John Hooker, to Rev. Thomas Hooker, who left Boston in 1635 to lead the settlement of Hartford, Connecticut.

Upon Rawson's death in 1693 he was buried in the Old Granary Cemetery near Rawson's Lane (later renamed Bromfield Street, which it remains today). No recognizable marker identifies the grave, but other gravestones still visible in that cemetery honor Samuel Adams and the victims of the Boston Massacre.

Edward Rawson
  Born April 16, 1615 Gillingham, Dorsetshire, England
  Died August 27, 1693 Boston, Massachusetts
Rachel (Perne)
  Born 1619 Blackmoor Vail, Dorsetshire, England
  Died October 11, 1677 Boston, Massachusetts

William Rawson was the seventh born of the twelve children of Edward and Rachel, but the eldest of the only two sons who did not return to England. The other, his brother Grindal, became a well-regarded minister who preached to the native tribes in their own language and served between 1680 and 1715 at the First Church in Mendon. William is described by the *Rawson Family Memoir* as "educated to a mercantile life" and as a "prominent merchant and an importer of foreign goods" who maintained a dry goods store near his father's home in Boston. In a genealogy of his in-laws, the Glover family, from the 19th century, William is characterized as "a wealthy merchant of Boston, of distinguished family and connections."

He married Anne Glover of Dorchester in 1673; she was the granddaughter of John Glover who arrived with Winthrop's first ships in 1630 and who moved from Charlestown to Dorchester in 1636. The Glover genealogy[7] provides this glowing description: "Mrs. Rawson is said to have been a lady of rare gifts and accomplishments, and inherited a portion of her mother's comeliness and grace. She had the advantages of a superior education, under the care of her grandmother..." The couple remained in Boston until 1689, when they moved first to Dorchester and later to nearby Braintree where William purchased land that once belonged to his great-uncle, the Rev. John Wilson. The *Rawson Family Memoir* relates that this land, next to the homestead of Josiah Quincy (an Adams ancestor), was known for generations as the "Ancient Rawson Farm." William and Anne had twenty children over a twenty-four year period, of whom only ten survived to adulthood.

William Rawson
    Born May 21, 1651 Boston, Massachusetts
    Died September 20, 1726 Braintree, Massachusetts
Anne (Glover)
    Born 1656 Dorchester, Massachusetts
    Died 1730 Braintree, Massachusetts

The second **William Rawson** was the eighth born but the first of his parents' twenty children to survive to adulthood. A Harvard College graduate, he followed his uncle, the Rev. Grindal Rawson, and his own brother, Nathaniel, out of Braintree to Mendon where, according to the *Rawson Family Memoir*, he was appointed a selectman in 1729 and town clerk in 1731. He also kept the school at various times. His wife Sarah Crosby was the daughter of early settler Simon Crosby, who had moved to Billerica from Braintree. They had eight children, of whom at least three died young.

William Rawson (sometimes called "Captain")
    Born December 2, 1682 Braintree, Massachusetts
    Died October 1769 Mendon, Massachusetts
Sarah (Crosby)
    Born July 27, 1684 Billerica, Massachusetts
    Died Unknown

The third consecutive **William Rawson** also served various roles in Mendon over the years, including town treasurer in 1734 and town clerk in 1740. The *Rawson Family Memoir* quotes a description of him as "a distinguished lawyer, and considered a man of learning in his day."
His wife, Margaret Cook, was a great-granddaughter of two of the founders of Mendon, Walter Cook and Ferdinando Thayer. William and Margaret had eight children; one of their sons, another William, died at Crown Point, New York in the French and Indian War in 1756.

William Rawson
    Born February 20, 1711 or 1712 Mendon, Massachusetts
    Died 1790 Mendon, Massachusetts
Margaret Cook
    Born December 18, 1711 Mendon, Massachusetts
    Died Unknown

Edward Rawson was the fifth son of William and Margaret and lived his entire life in Mendon, the third Rawson generation there. Married to Sarah Sadler, he worked as a farmer and a farrier in town. The couple had eight children. One, born in April 1775 amidst rising patriotic fervor in New England, they named Liberty. Edward Rawson is buried in the Old Cemetery in Mendon, and his grave bears a "Son of the American Revolution" marker.

Edward Rawson
  Born July 25, 1744 Mendon, Massachusetts
  Died June 16, 1823 Mendon, Massachusetts
Sarah (Sadler)
  Born 1742 Upton, Massachusetts
  Died October 19, 1814 Mendon, Massachusetts

Leonard Rawson broke the line of Rawsons who remained settled in Mendon by migrating 160 miles northwest to Pittsford, Vermont in 1800. As described earlier, a number of Leonard's first cousins had already made similar moves from central Massachusetts to lower Vermont. He bought land in Pittsford, then met and married Lydia Hitchcock. The daughter of John Hitchcock[8] who had brought his family north from Saybrook, Connecticut in 1785, Lydia died in Pittsford in 1817, the end of the infamous "Year without a Summer." One daughter died in 1818. Leonard's death followed Lydia's four years later. Both are buried in the Meeting House cemetery in Pittsford. They left as orphans two sons and four daughters, who may have been cared for by their uncle and aunt David and Abigail (Hitchcock) Hall; she was Lydia's sister and the Halls also lived in Pittsford after 1803.

Leonard Rawson
  Born August 23, 1771 Mendon, Massachusetts
  Died December 27, 1821 Pittsford, Vermont
Lydia (Hitchcock)
  Born September 6, 1776 Sommers, Connecticut
  Died February 2, 1817 Pittsford, Vermont

Edward Rawson, one of the young orphans (he was only ten when his father died), became part of the great migration of New Englanders to the states carved out of the Old Northwest Territory, especially after the opening of the Erie Canal in 1825. He showed up in Michigan records as a landowner, together with a David Hall (also from Vermont and probably Edward's first cousin's husband), in York, Michigan Territory in 1835. [9]

Edward married Sarah Newell Spalding, whose father John had brought his family west from Fort Ann, New York a few years earlier. Edward died in 1847 at the age of just 35; his gravestone can be found in the old Spaulding Cemetery in Milan, Michigan.

Edward Rawson
  Born April 22, 1811 Pittsford, Vermont
  Died March 17, 1847 York (Milan), Michigan
Sarah Newell (Spalding)
  Born February 10, 1820 Fort Ann, New York
  Died Unknown

John Spalding Rawson farmed land in southern Michigan near where he was born in 1841. One of three children of Edward and Sarah and their only son, he was just five years old when his father died. John and his first wife, Lucy Spaulding, had two children before she died young. His second wife also died in her thirties and he married a third time.

John Spalding Rawson
  Born October 9, 1841 Milan, Michigan
  Died August 30, 1916 Toledo, Ohio
Lucy (Spaulding)
  Born June 1, 1843 Whitehall, Michigan
  Died July 11, 1875 Milan, Michigan

L ike his father John, **Elson Frank Rawson** lived his entire life in southern Michigan not far from the Ohio line and the city of Toledo. He worked in Toledo as a letter carrier and also spent time there as the motorman of a trolley car. Later remembered by his family as a stern man, he married Minnie Ann McClarren who bore nine children. He is buried in Toledo.

Elson Frank Rawson
  Born June 10, 1873 Milan, Michigan
  Died March 31, 1956 Bedford, Michigan
Minnie Ann (McClarren)
  Born July 16, 1877 Wauseon, Ohio
  Died November 20, 1944 Bedford, Michigan

H ubert Graydon Rawson lived his entire life in Temperance, Michigan, just across the Ohio border and Toledo. The second of nine children of Elson and Minnie Ann, he married Rhoda May Dull in 1924. Her family had come to southern Michigan from Pennsylvania and Ohio. Raising vegetables and chickens behind their house, the couple helped their neighbors and extended family to scrape through the Depression. Hubert worked as an internal auditor for the local utility company, Toledo Edison. He lost his wife early to cancer while two of their four children were still young, but he never remarried. After retiring he joined his sister Jeannette in beginning to assemble from family bibles and records a genealogy of family connections.

Hubert Graydon Rawson
  Born August 8, 1904 Toledo, Ohio
  Died January 4, 1976 Temperance, Michigan
Rhoda May (Dull)
  Born June 21, 1904 Temperance, Michigan
  Died July 4, 1948 Toledo, Ohio

The next Rawson to undertake a major move, **Harold Bert Rawson** was the eldest of two sons (with Robert) and two daughters (Verna and Donna) born to Hubert and Rhoda. Raised in the Depression but fortunate to have a father who worked throughout those hard years, Hal served briefly in the Navy as World War II wound down, graduated from the University of Toledo in 1950 as an electrical engineer and married Joyce Reiter of Toledo whom he had met in college. (Unlike Hal's family roots in the Puritan Migration of the 1630s, Joyce Reiter's grandparents on both her father's side (Reiter) and her mother's side (Jankowski) reflected a different American immigration archetype. Instead of Puritan New England, they came to the United States in the 1880s and 1890s from central and eastern Europe through Ellis Island.)

The couple moved east when Hal was hired by AT&T's Western Electric in New York City, and later relocated first to Newark, New Jersey and then to suburban Florham Park, New Jersey after his transfer to Bell Telephone Laboratories. They raised four children (including the author) in their Forest Drive home. After his retirement from Bell Labs in 1985, Hal and his brother Robert turned in a serious way to the joint project of building on the family research that their father Hubert had launched in his own retirement years earlier. Harold and Joyce were interred in Madison, New Jersey, next to Florham Park.

Harold Bert Rawson
    Born October 15, 1925 Temperance, Michigan
    Died December 11, 2002 Parsippany, NJ
Joyce Marie (Reiter)
    Born August 15, 1929 Toledo, Ohio
    Died December 15, 1997 Florham Park, NJ

---

[1] This particular line of Rawsons, from Secretary Edward Rawson to the author, is obviously just one of many hundreds of lines that descended and branched from the Secretary. Other Rawson lines each provide their

own stories, many of which no doubt are more compelling than the one described here. But the history that underlies their various stories, as described here, is common to them all. Appendix Two seeks to provide a broader portrayal of these branches through the first seven generations, based on the information provided in the *Rawson Family Memoir* of 1875.

[2] *New England Journal of History*, Fall 1999.

[3] Id.

[4] The building was noteworthy enough that it was one of only a few structures represented at the edge of the royal forest on a 1624 map of the area. *See* generally Porter, pp. 95–102, 114.

[5] Currier, pp. 73–75; Coffin, p. 46.

[6] The wood frame Old South Church of 1669, at Washington and Milk Streets, was replaced by the Old South Meeting House in 1729, and by the New Old South Church at Boylston and Dartmouth Streets in 1875. Whitehill, *Boston*, pp. 32, 167, 245.

[7] *Genealogy of the Glover Family*, at pp. 210, 217. Anne Glover is also said to have "had a Negro," either an enslaved woman or a servant, named Dorcas. America's original sin of slavery reached even to the parlors of Boston.

[8] The progenitor of the Hitchcock family was Matthias Hitchcock, who came to Boston in 1635 and became one of the earliest settlers of New Haven, Connecticut, in 1639.

[9] There were several David Halls in the Pittsford area, creating a confusing situation. This David Hall was not the uncle of Edward Rawson in Pittsford, nor his son David Hall (Edward Rawson's first cousin), but rather another David Hall who in 1817 married the first David Hall's daughter Abigail (who was named for her mother, Edward Rawson's aunt Abigail (Hitchcock) Hall). It was likely this David Hall (Edward's first cousin's husband) who purchased land together with Edward Rawson and who also moved to Michigan in the 1830s.

APPENDIX TWO

AN ANALYSIS OF RAWSON MIGRATIONS

The particular line of Rawson descendants whose migration is the focus of this work (Edward, William, William, William, Edward, Leonard, Edward) is only one of hundreds that could be highlighted. For the same reason, the migration path described (Boston, Mendon MA, Pittsford VT, Milan MI), while unique to this line, is one of many paths that carried the Rawson family to different destinations over the first two hundred years after Secretary Edward Rawson's arrival. The revised *Rawson Family Memoir* from 1875 contains a wealth of genealogical data through seven generations and partially into an eighth. Even recognizing that family genealogies of this type are subject to errors and omissions, the data can be used to look for patterns in the directions chosen by individual family members.

The information provided in this Appendix Two is based on an analysis of the entries of the *Rawson Family Memoir*, which covers a period from roughly 1636 to 1875. The settlement location information is described here generation by generation from the first to the seventh, followed by a chart tracking the changes over time. A state-by-state table summarizing the information for the seventh generation (the largest and last to be included in the *Rawson Family Memoir*) is also included in this Appendix.

First Generation: As described in Appendix One, Edward Rawson landed in Massachusetts and stayed there for the rest of his life, living first in Newbury and then in Boston.

Massachusetts 1 person

Second Generation: Three of Secretary Edward Rawson's sons returned to England, joining a sister left behind when her parents emigrated and another who returned to England later; what little information the *Rawson Family Memoir* provides about his five other daughters suggests that all lived and died in the greater Boston area. Almost all of the entries, therefore, relate to Secretary Rawson's sons William and Grindal and their descendants. William remained in Boston for a number of years before moving to that part of Braintree, Massachusetts which later became Quincy. Grindal relocated to Mendon, Massachusetts to spend his life in ministry there.

Massachusetts	2

Third Generation: There are 12 entries in the third generation for whom settlement location information is provided. Two of these remained in the Boston/Braintree/Quincy area, while eight settled in Mendon. One moved to Milton, Massachusetts, and another became the first Rawson descendant to move out of Massachusetts and into Connecticut.

Massachusetts	11
Connecticut	1

Fourth Generation: Substantial movement begins in the fourth generation (roughly 1730 to 1770), for which 29 records provide settlement information. Although several descendants remained near Boston (five) or near Mendon (seven), twelve relocated to other towns in Massachusetts and five more left for other parts of New England, including Rhode Island, New Hampshire and Connecticut.

Massachusetts	24
Connecticut	2
Rhode Island	2
New Hampshire	1

Fifth Generation: This is the break-out generation (approximately 1750 to 1790), in which more than half of the 92 descendants are identified as making moves beyond Massachusetts. Nearly one-third (31) moved to other parts of New England (the largest number to Maine with 14). And one-fifth (20) settled outside of New England, largely in New York (13) but including some as far away as Louisiana (after 1840), Georgia, Ohio, Michigan and Virginia.

Massachusetts	41
Maine	14
New York	13
Rhode Island	7
Vermont	4
Connecticut	3
New Hampshire	3
Ohio	2
Georgia	2
Louisiana, Michigan, Virginia	1 each

Sixth Generation: The Rawson diaspora continued to grow, as the number of descendants living outside of New England approached one-half (96) of the members of the sixth generation for whom location information is available (197). New York state was by far the largest destination (60), but by this time (approximately 1800 to 1840) there were Rawsons in Illinois, Indiana, Iowa, Mississippi, Wisconsin and Canada, among other places. Only 43 (21.8%) of the sixth generation remained in Massachusetts, and another 58 (29.4%) settled in other parts of New England, especially Maine (19) and Vermont (16). The ancestral home areas of greater Boston (1) and Mendon (16) had largely lost their hold on the family.

New York	60
Massachusetts	43
Maine	19
Vermont	16
Ohio	15
Connecticut	11

Michigan	9
Rhode Island	7
New Hampshire	5
Illinois	4
Indiana	2
Wisconsin	2
Iowa, Pennsylvania, Mississippi and Canada	1 each

Seventh Generation: The *Rawson Family Memoir*, published in 1875, carries its records to the seventh generation (with only a handful thrown in from the eighth). Because this is the largest and last set of records, a more detailed analysis of this generation is provided here.

Destination Table for the Seventh Generation

Massachusetts	60	22.3%
Vermont	22	8.2%
Rhode Island	11	4.1%
Connecticut	9	3.3%
New Hampshire	3	1.1%
Maine	0	0%
Total New England	*105*	*39.0%*
New York	51	18.9%
Pennsylvania	1	0.3%
Total Mid-Atlantic	*52*	*19.2%*
Michigan	27	10.0%
Ohio	20	7.4%
Wisconsin	16	5.9%
Illinois	15	5.6%
Indiana	7	2.6%
Total Northwest	*85*	*31.6%*
Iowa	7	2.6%

Minnesota	4	1.5%
Kansas	3	1.1%
Georgia	3	1.1%
Kentucky	2	0.7%
Utah	2	0.7%

Arkansas, California, Missouri, Maryland, South
Carolina and Canada   1 each

Total other places	*27*	*10.0%*

A closer look at this list of 25 destinations shows that the five largest recipients of Rawson immigrants accounted for fully two-thirds of the 269 people in the seventh generation (roughly 1830 to 1875) for whom settlement location data is provided in the *Rawson Family Memoir*:

Massachusetts	60	22.3%
New York	51	18.9%
Michigan	27	10.0%
Vermont	22	8.2%
Ohio	20	7.4%
Total top five states	*180*	*66.9%*

Breaking the data on seventh generation descendants into the lines that begin with Secretary Edward Rawson's sons, William and Grindal, yields very interesting results. The following table shows that the descendants of Grindal, generally speaking, stayed closer to home than William's descendants did:

	William (191)		Grindal (78)	
Massachusetts	25	13.1%	35	44.9%
New England	58	30.4%	47	60.2%
(Including MA)				
New York	40	20.9%	11	14.1%
Northwest Territory	66	34.6%	19	24.4%
Other	27	14.1%	1	1.3%

In short, nearly two-thirds of Grindal's descendants to the seventh generation stayed in New England, while more than two-thirds of William's descendants to the seventh generation settled outside New England, including some as far away as Arkansas, Georgia, Utah and California. The homes of the first and second generations, Boston (4) and Mendon (13), accounted for less than 7% of seventh generation Rawson descendants.

The following chart tracks the growth and decline of Rawson descendants in various geographic areas across all seven generations covered by the *Rawson Family Memoir*. Unfortunately, no data is available for the subsequent six or seven generations since 1875, although one might reasonably expect that the "Outside N.E." line would continue upward before reaching a plateau.

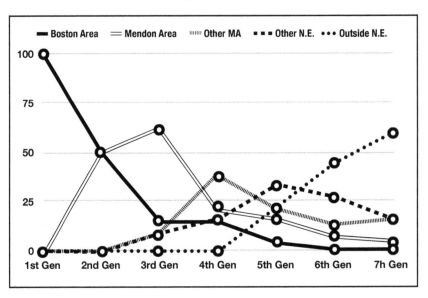

Appendix Three

Historical Timeline

Date and Event:

1600–1604
King James I on the throne

1605–1609
Gunpowder Plot to assassinate James fails
Jamestown, Virginia settled
Samuel de Champlain in Canada
Henry Hudson explores New Amsterdam

1610–1614

1615–1619
Edward Rawson born in Gillingham, England
First enslaved Africans brought to Virginia

1620–1624
Mayflower lands at Provincetown and then Plymouth
Dorchester Company settlement at Cape Ann
Robert Gorges company settlement at Weymouth
King Charles I on the throne

1625–1629
King Charles dissolves Parliament
Massachusetts Bay Company organized in London

1630–1634
Winthrop fleet and *Mary & John* landings in MBC (to 1640)

1635–1639

Edward Rawson in Newbury MBC

Roger Williams banished from MBC, founds Rhode Island

Pequot War in New England

1640–1644

Civil war begins in England between royal and parliamentary forces

1645–1649

King Charles I executed

1650–1654

Edward Rawson becomes Secretary, MBC

Parliament wins the Civil War; England becomes a
    Commonwealth

Oliver Cromwell named Lord Protector; Parliament dissolved

1655–1659

Petition for Mendon settlement

1660–1664

King Charles II and the Restoration of the crown

First settlers in Mendon

1665–1669

Black Plague hits London

English expel the Dutch from New Amsterdam

Great Fire destroys much of London

French fort at Isle Le Motte on L. Champlain
    (first European outpost in Vermont)

1670–1674

1675–1679

King Philip's War in Plymouth and MBC

Mendon attacked and destroyed, later resettled

1680–1684

Rev. Grindal Rawson to Mendon

King James II on the throne
LaSalle explores and claims the Mississippi River lands for
    France

1685–1689
Colonies reorganized into Dominion of New England
England's Glorious Revolution of 1688 deposes James II
Colonial authorities oust royal Governor Andros

1690–1694
War in Europe
King William and Queen Mary on the throne
King William's War in America
William Rawson (1) to Braintree
Plymouth merged into Massachusetts Bay Colony

1695–1699
MBC designates "frontier towns" including Mendon

1700–1704
Queen Anne on the throne
War in Europe
Queen Anne's War in America
Indian raid on Deerfield MA
French trading post at Detroit

1705–1709

1710–1714
William Rawson (2) in Mendon
William Rawson (3) in Mendon

1715–1719
King George I on the throne

1720–1724
Grey Lock's War in New England
English build Fort Dummer (first English outpost in
    Vermont)

1725–1729

King George II on the throne
Edward Rawson (2) in Mendon

1730–1734

French build Fort St. Frederic at Crown Point

1735–1739

1740–1744

War in Europe
King George's War in America

1745–1749

First New Hampshire (NH) Grants made

1750–1754

War in Europe
French & Indian War begins in America (to 1763)
Washington surrenders Fort Necessity to French

1755–1759

King George III on the throne

1760–1764

French lose Lake Champlain to Britain
Britain takes Canada
Pittsford founded as a NH Grant
Treaty of Paris ends French & Indian War
Proclamation of 1763 seeks to limit western settlements
Pontiac's War in the Ohio country

1765–1769

Parliament passes the Stamp Act over colonial objections

1770–1774

The Boston Massacre
Boston Tea Party

1775–1779
Revolutionary War begins at Concord and Lexington (to 1783)
Declaration of Independence by the United States
Vermont declares its independence

1780–1784
Peace of Paris recognizes American independence

1785–1789
President George Washington
Northwest Ordinance passed

1790–1794
Vermont statehood
Battle of Fallen Timbers in Ohio
Treaty of Greenville ends Indian war in the Northwest

1795–1799
Jay Treaty between U.S. and Great Britain
President John Adams

1800–1804
Leonard Rawson to Pittsford VT
President Thomas Jefferson
Napoleonic Wars begin
Louisiana Purchase from France
Ohio statehood

1805–1809
Michigan territorial status
Napoleon becomes Emperor in France
British win the Battle of Trafalgar against the French
President James Madison

1810–1814
Battle of Tippecanoe in Indiana
War of 1812 (to 1815)
British burn the White House
Battle of Lake Erie
Battle of Plattsburgh Bay, Lake Champlain

1815–1819
Tecumseh killed at Thames, Canada
Napoleon returns from exile, is defeated at Waterloo
Mount Tambora volcano erupts in Indonesia
"Year Without a Summer" in New England
President James Monroe
First steamboats on the Great Lakes

1820–1824
King George IV on the throne
President John Quincy Adams

1825–1829
Erie Canal opens
President Andrew Jackson

1830–1834
Indian Removal Act signed into law
Queen Victoria on the throne
"Toledo War" border dispute
Black Hawk's War ends

1835–1839
Edward Rawson (3) to Milan MI
President Martin Van Buren
Panic of 1837
Michigan statehood

AUTHOR'S NOTE

This project began in conversations with my father, Hal Rawson. After his retirement from Bell Labs in 1985, he developed a passion for genealogy. Building on work by his aunt and his own father, Dad assembled a data base of names, dates and places, which he stored on his little Commodore computer. He recruited his brother Bob into the effort, and they divided the family into paternal and maternal lines for investigation. Without access to a world wide web in those years, they scoured libraries and tramped through cemeteries, sharing findings and comparing notes from time to time. Dad approached genealogy as if it were one of the jigsaw puzzles he so loved, searching patiently for just the right piece to fit into its unique opening. Every new entry was a source of satisfaction, every missing link a frustration.

We talked about the fact that our forebears had not stayed in the northeast, where our earliest immigrant forefather Secretary Edward Rawson of the Massachusetts Bay Colony had made his home in 1636. Instead, over a period of seven generations, our particular line of Rawsons moved away from Boston into central Massachusetts, up to Vermont and then out to Michigan. I said that, although the search for connections was fun and interesting, I was even more intrigued by the moves our ancestors had made. Even though it was impossible to know what was in the mind of each of these westerly migrating Rawsons, there had to be clues in the story of their times from which reasonable inferences could be drawn. If we could understand what was happening in their world, we might be able to discern the most likely reasons for their relocations. I told Dad *that* was a book I would like to write someday.

Dad died in 2002, leaving behind wonderful family memories as well as binders full of computer printouts of genealogical data. After my retirement from practicing law, I began to read about the Great Puritan Migration, the French and Indian War, the Erie Canal and many other topics to help me understand the forces that could have influenced our Rawson forebears between 1636 and 1836. I devoured the work of migration historians like Frederick Merk, Bernard Bailyn and David Hackett Fischer. Reading became note-taking, which turned into outlines, which led to writing. Before long, I dared to think that even a history loving non-historian like I am might be able to put together a narrative worth reading. The births of three grandsons gave the project greater urgency. I have no illusions that the interested audience will be much wider than my own family and good friends. But it gives me great satisfaction to think that someday, perhaps a hundred years hence, someone descended from the Secretary and me (or not) might find this work on an antiquarian book shelf, page through it, learn something new and be glad I had taken the time to tell this particular Rawson story in its historical context.

As a writer untutored in historical research methods or protocols, I have relied heavily on secondary materials rather than original research. Every effort has been made to acknowledge my sources, to make fair use of published material and to provide attribution wherever appropriate. I regret any lapses in these efforts, as well as the mistakes I'm sure to have made in places. Although the work is non-fiction, it will be clear to readers that, in the case of three short vignettes introducing chapters, I have taken the liberty of imagining a scene and describing the thoughts of particular ancestors; I hope these small dramatic creations will not undercut the reader's confidence in the accuracy of the account overall.

I am grateful to the many people in libraries and museums who have helped in my search for useful material, particularly in Gillingham, Dorchester, Weymouth, Boston, Mendon, Pittsford, Toledo and Milan, as well as to those who have read over and commented on drafts of the work. Readers who know me well will not be surprised at the inclusion of historical episodes or anecdotes relating to places of importance in my life: Toledo (Put-in-Bay, Turtle Island, the Toledo War); Lake Champlain (Westport, Arnold Bay, Crown Point, Vergennes); and, of course, my hometown of Florham Park, New Jersey. And it's been fun to walk on what used to be called Rawson's Lane near Boston Common, to find the land in Pittsford, Vermont where a Rawson house once sat, and to stand at the gate to Rawson's Court in Gillingham, England.

In fact, this entire work might fairly be described with a phrase from my favorite non-fiction author, the nonpareil John McPhee, in his recent *Draft No. 4* (at pp. 56–57): I've "include[d] what interests me and exclude[d] what doesn't interest me." All with an eye on teaching a few interesting things to my grandsons and perhaps even to theirs.

Finally, I want to thank my wife, Lois Rawson, for her patience and unwavering support as I stole time over several years to work on my research and writing, and as we traveled to many out of the way places to gather information I needed. The families of Lois and the other women who married into our Rawson clan over many generations—Browns and Reiters, Dulls and McLarrens, Spaldings and Spauldings, Hitchcocks and Sadlers, Cooks and Crosbys, Glovers and Pernes and Wilsons—are an equally important but largely untold part of the Rawson story. Maybe there's another book in there somewhere.

Richard Rawson
Alexandria, Virginia 2019

SELECTIVE BIBLIOGRAPHY

Allen, Thomas B. *Tories: Fighting for the King in America's First Civil War*. New York: HarperCollins, 2010.

Bailyn, Bernard. *The Barbarous Years: The Peopling of British North America: The Conflict of Civilizations, 1600–1675*. New York: Alfred A. Knopf, 2012.

Bailyn, Bernard. *The Peopling of British North America: An Introduction*. New York: Vintage Books, 1986.

Bailyn, Bernard. *Voyagers to the West: A Passage in the Peopling of America on the Eve of the Revolution*. New York: Vintage Books, 1986.

Beer, G.L. *The Origins of the British Colonial System, 1578–1660*. New York: 1908.

Bellico, Russell P. *Sails and Steam in the Mountains: A Maritime and Military History of Lake George and Lake Champlain*. Fleischmanns, New York: Purple Mountain Press, 1992.

Blois, John T. *Gazetteer of the State of Michigan*. Detroit: Sydney L. Rood & Co., New York: Robinson, Pratt And Co., 1838.

Bobrick, Benson. *Angel in the Whirlwind: The Triumph of the American Revolution*. New York: Simon & Schuster, 1997.

Borneman, Walter R. *The French and Indian War*. New York: Harper Collins, 2006.

Brown, Dee. *Bury My Heart At Wounded Knee*. New York: Henry Holt Books, 1970.

Burnet, Jacob. *Notes on the Early Settlement of the North-Western Territory*. New York: Arno Press, 1975.

Calloway, Colin G. *Western Abenakis of Vermont, 1600–1800*. Norman: University of Oklahoma Press, 1990.

Caverly, A.M. *History of the Town of Pittsford, Vt*. Rutland: Tuttle and Co., 1872.

Chartrand, Rene. *The Forts of New France in Northeast America 1600–1763*. Oxford: Osprey Publishing, Inc. 2008.

Chernow, Ron. *Washington, A Life*. New York: The Penguin Press, 2010.

Clapp, Ebenezer Jr. *History of the Town of Dorchester, Massachusetts*. Boston: Dorchester Antiquarian and Historical Society, 1859.

Crane, E.B. (Editor) *The Rawson Family: A Revised Memoir of Edward Rawson, Secretary of the Colony of Massachusetts Bay*. Worcester: Private Publication, 1875.

Currier, John J. *History of Newbury 1635–1902*. Boston: Damrell & Upham, 1902.

Drake, Samuel G. *The History and Antiquities of Boston*. Boston: Luther Stephens, 1856.

Fischer, David Hackett. *Albion's Seed: Four British Folkways in America*. New York: Oxford University Press, 1989.

Fischer, David Hackett and Kelly, James C. *Bound Away: Virginia and the Westward Movement*. Charlottesville and London: University of Virginia Press, 2000.

Hill, Ralph Nading. *Lake Champlain: Key to Liberty*. Woodstock, New York: The Countryman Press, 1976.

Hurt, R. Douglas. *The Ohio Frontier: Crucible of the Old Northwest, 1720–1830*. Bloomington & Indianapolis: Indiana University Press, 1996.

Imbrie, John and Imbrie, Katherine Palmer. *Ice Ages: Solving the Mystery*. Cambridge: Harvard University Press, 1979.

Kelso, William M. *Jameston: The Truth Revealed*. Charlottesville: University of Virginia Press, 2017.

Laramie, Michael G. *By Wind and Iron*. Yardley, Pennsylvania: Westholme Publishing, LLC, 2015.

Lepore, Jill. *The Name of War: King Philip's War and the Origins of American Identity*. New York: Vintage Books, 1998.

Lewis, Kenneth E. *West to Far Michigan: Settling the Lower Peninsula, 1815–1860*. East Lansing: Michigan State University Press, 2002.

Mann, Charles C. *1491: New Revelations of the Americas Before Columbus.* New York: Vintage Books, 2005.

McPhee, John. *Draft No. 4: On the Writing Process.* New York: Farrar, Straus and Giroux, 2017.

Mello, Robert A. *Moses Robinson and Founding of Vermont.* Barre and Montpelier: The Vermont Historical Society, 2014.

Merk, Frederick. *History of the Westward Movement.* New York: Alfred A. Knopf, 1978.

Middlekauff, Robert. *The Glorious Cause: The American Revolution, 1763–1789.* New York: Oxford University Press, 2005.

Morison, Samuel Eliot. *The Oxford History of the American People.* New York: Oxford University Press, 1965.

Morison, Samuel Eliot. *The European Discovery of America: The Northern Voyages.* New York: Oxford University Press, 1971.

Philbrick, Nathaniel. *Mayflower.* New York: Penguin Group, 2006.

Philbrick, Nathaniel. *Valiant Ambition: George Washington, Benedict Arnold, and the Fate of the American Revolution.* New York: Penguin Random House LLC, 2016.

Porter, John. *Gillingham's Royal Forest.* Gillingham: The Gillingham Museum and Local History Society, 2014.

Rybczynski, Witold. *City Life.* New York: Touchstone, 1995.

Schultz, Eric B. and Tougias, Michael J. *King Philip's War.* Woodstock, Vermont: The Countryman Press, 1999.

Sherman, Michael, Sessions, Gene, and Potash, P. Jeffrey. *Freedom and Unity: A History of Vermont.* Barre, Vermont: Vermont Historical Society, 2004.

Skaggs, David Curtis and Altoff, Gerard T. *A Signal Victory: The Lake Erie Campaign 1812–1813.* Annapolis, Maryland: Bluejacket Books, 1997.

Smith, H.P. and Rann, W.S. *History of Rutland County Vermont.* Syracuse, New York: D. Mason and Co., 1886.

Spencer, Charles. *Killers of the King.* New York/London: Bloomsbury Press, 2014.

Srinivasan, Bhu. *Americana: A 400-Year History of American Capitalism.* New York: Penguin Random House LLC, 2017.

Taylor, Alan. *American Colonies: The Settling of North America.* New York: The Penguin Group, 2001.

Teaford, Jon C. *The American Suburb: The Basics.* New York/London: Rutledge, 2008.

Toqueville, Alexis de. *Democracy in America, Vols I and II.* New York: Alfred A. Knopf, Inc, 1994. (Reprint)

Ward, Michael K. *Rebecca Rawson: Portrait of a Daughter of the Puritan Elite in the Massachusetts Bay Colony.* The New England Journal of History, Volume 56 No. 1 Fall 1999, pp. 22–35.

Washington, George. *Writings.* New York: Literary Classics of the United States, 1997.

Weiss, Eleanor. *Saga of a Crossroads: Florham Park.* Historical Society of Florham Park, 1988.

White, Theodore. *The Making of the President 1960.* New York: Atheneum Publishers, 1961.

Whittier, John Greenleaf. *Leaves From Margaret Smith's Journal In The Province of Massachusetts Bay, 1678–1679.* Boston: Ticknor, Reed and Fields, 1849.

Wright, Ronald. *Stolen Continents: 500 Years of Conquest and Resistance in the Americas.* Boston/New York: Houghton Mifflin Company, 1992.

INDEX OF HISTORICAL NAMES

ABOUT THE AUTHOR

A retired lawyer with an avid interest in American history, Richard Rawson has been a corporate general counsel, a law school professor, a trustee of both Rutgers University and Drew University, and a recipient of awards for his work to help diversify the legal profession.

Richard is an 11th generation descendant of Edward Rawson, who was part of the Great Puritan Migration to North America in the 1630s and who served as secretary of the Massachusetts Bay Colony between 1650 and 1686. A long time New Jerseyan, the author now lives in Alexandria, Virginia. *Migration* is his first book.

Published by E.L.F. Book Enterprises
Alexandria, Virginia

ISBN: 978-0-578-46229-5 Hardbound
ISBN: 978-0-578-46334-6 Softbound

Epilogue photo on page 101 by the author

Author photo by Casey Held Rawson

Maps by David Gordon

Cover image by Iurii Kovalenko©123rf.com

Portrait of Edward Rawson on page iv: Public Domain
http://illustrationarchive.cardiff.ac.uk/page_turner/000839767/000054/0

Book designed and produced
by Lucky Valley Press, Jacksonville, Oregon
www.luckyvalleypress.com

Printed in the United States of America on acid-free paper that meets the Sustainable Forestry Initiative® Chain-of-Custody Standards. www.sfiprogram.org

Titles, headers, map captions and display text are set in the Fell Types, late-17th Century typefaces digitally reproduced by Igino Marini. (iginomarini.com)

The body text is set in a modern digital version of Caslon, one of the most widely used typefaces in the 18th Century.